I0465461

JOHN EZRA BIEN

Path to Prosperity- Your Guide to Lifelong Wealth

Copyright © 2024 by John Ezra Bien

All rights reserved. No part of this publication may be reproduced, stored or transmitted in any form or by any means, electronic, mechanical, photocopying, recording, scanning, or otherwise without written permission from the publisher. It is illegal to copy this book, post it to a website, or distribute it by any other means without permission.

First edition

This book was professionally typeset on Reedsy.
Find out more at reedsy.com

Contents

Introduction

Welcome to Path to Prosperity: Your Guide to Lifelong Wealth. In a world where financial security often feels like a distant dream, this book serves as your comprehensive guide to achieving and sustaining wealth through every stage of life. Imagine a future where money isn't a source of stress but a tool that empowers you to live freely—whether that's traveling the world, launching your own business, securing a comfortable retirement, or leaving a meaningful legacy for generations to come.

Building wealth in today's ever-evolving economy requires more than just saving diligently or relying on a single income stream. True prosperity is built on a mindset that embraces continuous learning, adaptability, and proactive financial strategies. Path to Prosperity isn't just about reaching a financial milestone; it's about mastering the essential skills and principles that will guide you toward lasting success, no matter what life throws your way.

What You'll Discover in This Book

This book takes you on a practical, step-by-step journey, breaking down wealth-building strategies into actionable chapters that you can apply immediately. Each section is designed to equip you with the tools necessary to build a solid financial foundation, generate diverse income streams, make strategic investments, and manage your money effectively. These aren't just short-term tips—they're skills that will continue to support and grow your wealth throughout your life.

A New Perspective on Wealth

Wealth is much more than just numbers in your bank account. It's a mindset, a way of living that gives you the freedom to pursue your passions, support the people you care about, and create lasting impact. True prosperity is a balance of financial well-being, personal growth, and the peace of mind that comes from being in control of your financial future. By the end of this book, you'll see wealth not as a destination, but as an ongoing journey that brings meaning and purpose to your life.

Why This Book is Different

Path to Prosperity provides a holistic view of wealth-building, covering every essential aspect of personal finance. From budgeting and saving to investing and building passive income, each chapter draws from proven strategies and the real-world experiences of successful individuals. Whether you're seeking to grow your wealth, protect it, or leave a legacy, this book offers practical advice and insights that are both straightforward and profound.

Throughout this guide, you'll learn how to cultivate financial discipline, harness new opportunities, and protect your wealth from risks. But most importantly, you'll learn how to align your financial decisions with your values, so that money becomes a tool to create the life you've always dreamed of.

A Path Suited to You

Whether you're just starting your career, looking to multiply your existing wealth, or planning for a secure retirement, Path to Prosperity is designed to meet you where you are. The chapters are tailored to provide actionable insights and strategies that are relevant to your current stage of life, ensuring that you can apply the concepts immediately to your unique situation. The tools you'll discover here are adaptable, transformative, and will serve you for years to come.

What You Stand to Gain

By the time you reach the end of this book, you'll have not only a deep understanding of how to build and preserve wealth, but also the confidence to make wise financial decisions that align with your personal goals. Each chapter will empower you to take control of your financial future and create a life of true abundance. This isn't about quick fixes or "get-rich-quick" schemes; it's about building steady, sustainable wealth over time.

Prepare to embark on a transformative journey that will change the way you think about, earn, invest, and enjoy money. Let's begin this exciting adventure toward lifelong prosperity.

The Power of Mindset in Building Wealth

U nlocking the Foundation of Prosperity

Wealth creation begins not with the numbers in your bank account or the investments in your portfolio but with something much more fundamental—your mindset. Everything you do, the choices you make, and the path you take in life is shaped by the way you think. It's this underlying thought process that determines the trajectory of your financial journey.

When we talk about wealth-building, the term "mindset" is often mentioned, but it is rarely given the attention it truly deserves. Your mindset is more than just a mental attitude. It's a core belief system that dictates how you approach challenges, setbacks, opportunities, and risks in the pursuit of prosperity. In this chapter, we'll explore how the right mindset can transform your financial future, leading you to a life of wealth and abundance.

* * *

The Relationship Between Mindset and Wealth

Wealth, in its truest form, is not just about accumulating money—it's about achieving financial freedom, autonomy, and security. But to get there, you must first understand that the greatest wealth-building tool is your own mindset. The way you perceive money, wealth, and financial success can significantly impact the outcomes of your efforts.

Take a moment to reflect: How do you feel about money? Do you view it as something scarce, something that is hard to earn, or do you see it as an abundant resource that flows freely to those who are wise enough to manage it? Your beliefs about money are the foundation upon which your wealth-building efforts are built.

The wealth mindset is characterized by several key beliefs and attitudes:

Abundance vs. Scarcity: Those with an abundance mindset believe there is always enough wealth to go around, and opportunities for prosperity are endless. On the other hand, a scarcity mindset can limit opportunities and hold people back from taking risks and making bold financial decisions.

Growth vs. Fixed Mindset: A growth-oriented mindset embraces challenges and sees failures as opportunities for learning and improvement. A fixed mindset, however, fears failure and avoids change, making it difficult to adapt in the face of evolving financial landscapes.

Delayed Gratification: Wealth builders understand that patience and self-discipline are necessary. They are willing to make short-term sacrifices to reap long-term rewards, such as saving, investing, and avoiding impulsive spending.

Self-Efficacy: Individuals with a wealth-building mindset believe they have control over their financial future. They take responsibility for their actions and seek continuous improvement rather than blaming external circumstances.

* * *

The Psychology of Wealth

At its core, building wealth is as much a psychological journey as it is a financial one. Your mind has the power to either propel you toward your goals or keep you stuck in a cycle of struggle. Psychology plays a crucial role in shaping how you deal with money, from how you handle your earnings to how you perceive your financial potential.

One of the most significant psychological barriers to wealth creation is fear. Fear of losing money, fear of failure, and fear of not being good enough can paralyze even the most promising individuals. To overcome these fears, it's essential to confront them directly and change your perception. Wealth creators are not fearless, but they choose to act despite their fears. They see risk as an opportunity to grow and take calculated chances that bring them closer to their financial goals.

Another psychological factor at play is the concept of self-worth.

Many people are subconsciously limited by their beliefs about what they deserve. If you don't believe you deserve wealth, your actions will reflect that belief. Building a wealth-oriented mindset involves changing your self-concept to one that believes you are worthy of financial success, which in turn influences your decisions, behaviors, and actions.

* * *

The Wealth Mindset Blueprint

Building the right mindset for wealth isn't an overnight process. It requires a sustained effort and a willingness to challenge your old beliefs. Here's a blueprint to develop a mindset that can support wealth creation:

1. Embrace Abundance
   Start by shifting from a scarcity mindset to an abundance mindset. Believe that there are limitless opportunities for wealth creation, and that your success does not diminish the success of others. Focus on possibilities instead of limitations.

2. Adopt a Growth Mindset
   Cultivate a mindset that thrives on challenges and views setbacks as opportunities to grow. Financial success is rarely achieved without experiencing failure at some point. Embrace mistakes, learn from them, and use those lessons to improve your future decisions.

3. Practice Patience and Delayed Gratification

Wealth is built over time, not overnight. Successful wealth-builders prioritize long-term gains over short-term pleasures. By practicing delayed gratification, you learn to invest in yourself and your future, often at the expense of immediate satisfaction.

4. Visualize Your Financial Goals

Visualization is a powerful tool that successful individuals use to manifest their goals. Spend time visualizing your financial success in vivid detail. Picture yourself achieving your wealth goals, experiencing the lifestyle you desire, and enjoying financial freedom.

5. Reprogram Negative Beliefs About Money

Identify any negative beliefs you may have about money and work to replace them with empowering thoughts. This could be a belief that money is the root of evil, that you aren't capable of achieving wealth, or that financial success is for others and not you.

6. Focus on Abundance in All Areas of Life

Wealth is not just about money—it's about a holistic sense of abundance. Focus on abundance in your health, relationships, career, and personal growth. When you align every area of your life with abundance, wealth naturally follows.

7. Take Responsibility for Your Financial Journey

Accept full responsibility for your financial situation, regardless of external circumstances. By taking ownership of your financial destiny, you empower yourself to make the necessary changes and take the right actions.

8. Seek Out Wealth Mentors
Surround yourself with individuals who have achieved the level of wealth you aspire to. Learn from their experiences, adopt their habits, and use their insights to refine your own wealth-building strategy.

* * *

Mindset Shifts for Overcoming Challenges

Wealth-building isn't without its challenges. Every path to prosperity will encounter obstacles, whether they're financial setbacks, market downturns, or personal doubts. But the key to overcoming these challenges lies in your ability to manage your mindset.

The first step is to accept failure as part of the process. Failure is not the end but rather a stepping stone on the path to success. It's not a reflection of your worth, but a reflection of your willingness to take risks and learn.

Next, embrace adaptability. Markets and opportunities evolve, and those who succeed are those who can pivot when necessary. The ability to adapt is a trait of wealthy individuals—they are constantly learning, changing, and adjusting their strategies to keep up with new trends.

Finally, remember the power of perseverance. Building wealth is a marathon, not a sprint. There will be ups and downs, but those who succeed are those who don't give up. Stay committed to your financial goals and trust the process.

* * *

The Key to Unlocking Your Wealth Potential

Your mindset is the most powerful tool you possess in your quest for wealth. By changing the way you think about money, opportunity, and success, you unlock the potential to achieve financial freedom. Developing a wealth-oriented mindset requires time, practice, and continuous effort, but it is the most important investment you can make in your future.

When you cultivate the right mindset, you will find that wealth is not something elusive or out of reach—it is a natural byproduct of the choices, actions, and beliefs you adopt every day. This mindset shift is the foundation on which your entire journey toward prosperity will be built.

Building a Solid Foundation

L aying the Groundwork for Financial Security

In your journey toward lifelong wealth, nothing is more essential than building a strong financial foundation. Just as a house relies on a sturdy base, financial security depends on a foundation that's stable, well-planned, and resilient against unexpected changes. This foundation begins with mastering the basics of money management, setting achievable goals, and developing habits that support long-term prosperity. In this chapter, we'll delve into these core principles and explore the steps to construct a financial base that will support and sustain your wealth over time.

* * *

Understanding Money Management: The Cornerstone of Wealth

Money management is not only about earning or saving but also about developing a system to allocate, monitor, and grow your finances. It involves creating a budget, tracking expenses, managing debt, and building savings. These practices may seem straightforward, yet they form the basis of sound financial health.

1. Budgeting

A budget is the framework for all financial decisions. By outlining your income, expenses, and goals, you gain a clear understanding of where your money goes each month. Effective budgeting isn't restrictive; rather, it empowers you to spend consciously and allocate funds where they'll be most productive.

2. Expense Tracking

Awareness is key to financial control. Track every dollar you spend for a few months, noting patterns in your spending behavior. Are there unnecessary expenses that could be minimized? Knowing where your money goes helps you identify areas for adjustment and ultimately directs more funds toward wealth-building activities.

3. Debt Management

Debt, especially high-interest debt, is one of the biggest obstacles to building wealth. Reducing debt should be a priority, whether it's credit card balances, student loans, or personal loans. Adopt a strategy—such as the snowball or avalanche method—to pay down debt efficiently. Once you're free of unnecessary debt, you can redirect those funds toward investments and savings.

4. Building an Emergency Fund

An emergency fund serves as a financial safety net. Life is unpredictable, and unexpected expenses are inevitable. Aim to set aside enough to cover three to six months' worth of living expenses. With this cushion, you're less likely to rely on debt during unforeseen events, protecting your financial health and stability.

* * *

Setting Clear Financial Goals

A wealth-building journey without clear goals is like navigating without a map. Financial goals provide purpose, focus, and motivation, guiding you toward the future you envision. When setting goals, it's essential to be specific and intentional, aligning each one with your long-term vision.

1. Short-Term Goals
These are immediate financial objectives, such as paying off credit card debt, establishing an emergency fund, or saving for a vacation. Short-term goals build momentum and encourage positive financial behaviors that support larger goals.

2. Mid-Term Goals
Mid-term goals typically span two to five years and may include saving for a home down payment, pursuing further education, or

purchasing a car. These goals require more significant planning and dedication, often involving consistent contributions and financial discipline.

3. Long-Term Goals

Long-term goals are your ultimate financial aspirations, such as achieving financial independence, securing retirement, or creating generational wealth. These goals demand patience, commitment, and a strategic approach to investing and saving.

4. The SMART Goal Framework

A useful framework for setting financial goals is SMART: Specific, Measurable, Achievable, Relevant, and Time-bound. SMART goals ensure clarity and accountability, making it easier to stay on track and monitor your progress.

* * *

Creating a Systematic Approach to Wealth-Building

Achieving financial security is not a one-time effort but a sustained, strategic process. Establishing systems for saving, investing, and managing finances will help automate your journey toward wealth.

1. Automate Savings

Setting up automatic transfers to savings and investment accounts is one of the simplest ways to build wealth consistently. By automating contributions, you eliminate the temptation to spend and ensure steady growth in your financial reserves.

2. Pay Yourself First

Prioritize your financial goals by allocating funds to savings and investments before addressing discretionary spending. This "pay yourself first" strategy reinforces your commitment to wealth-building and keeps financial goals at the forefront of your monthly budget.

3. Monitor and Adjust Regularly

Financial goals and circumstances change over time. Regularly review your progress and adjust your budget, savings plan, and investments as needed. Staying proactive and flexible allows you to adapt your foundation to evolving needs and opportunities.

* * *

Building Financial Habits for Stability and Growth

Creating lasting financial security requires developing habits that reinforce your foundation. These daily and monthly practices keep you on track, helping you make steady progress toward long-term wealth.

1. Consistent Saving

Saving consistently, even if the amount seems small, is a powerful wealth-building habit. Small amounts compounded over time add up and contribute significantly to your financial foundation. Develop the habit of setting aside a portion of every paycheck, even if it's just a small percentage.

2. Practicing Financial Discipline

Discipline in spending and saving is essential to financial success. This means resisting the urge to make impulse purchases, avoiding lifestyle inflation as your income grows, and adhering to your budget. Discipline reinforces your commitment to wealth-building.

3. Living Below Your Means

The practice of spending less than you earn is foundational to wealth accumulation. It allows you to allocate funds toward savings, investments, and debt reduction, accelerating your progress toward financial independence.

4. Mindful Spending

Every spending decision is an opportunity to assess value. Before making a purchase, consider whether it aligns with your goals and brings genuine value to your life. Mindful spending ensures that your financial choices reflect your priorities.

* * *

Avoiding Common Pitfalls in Financial Foundation Building

In building your financial foundation, it's essential to be aware of common mistakes that can hinder progress. Recognizing and avoiding these pitfalls strengthens your path to financial security.

1. Lifestyle Inflation

As income increases, many people raise their spending accordingly—a phenomenon known as lifestyle inflation. Instead of upgrading your lifestyle with each raise, allocate the extra income toward savings and investments, allowing your foundation to grow.

2. Neglecting Retirement Planning

One of the most significant financial mistakes is delaying retirement planning. The earlier you start, the more time your investments have to grow. Prioritize retirement savings and take advantage of compound growth to secure your future.

3. Over-Reliance on Debt

Debt can be an obstacle to financial security if not managed responsibly. Avoid accumulating unnecessary debt, and focus on using credit strategically for asset-building, such as real estate or business ventures, rather than consumer purchases.

4. Ignoring Financial Education

Financial literacy is an asset in wealth-building. Invest time in learning about personal finance, investing, and wealth-building strategies. The more informed you are, the better equipped you'll be to make sound financial decisions.

* * *

Laying the Foundation for Lasting Wealth

Building a solid financial foundation is the first and most crucial step in your journey to lifelong wealth. By mastering money management, setting clear financial goals, and adopting positive financial habits, you create a base that supports and sustains growth. This foundation is not only about the numbers—it's about establishing a mindset of discipline, consistency, and mindful decision-making.

Your financial foundation will serve as the bedrock upon which you construct your wealth. As you progress, each goal achieved and habit formed strengthens this base, bringing you closer to financial independence and prosperity. The journey to wealth may be long, but with a solid foundation, it becomes a steady, manageable, and fulfilling path.

Understanding Income Streams

The Power of Multiple Income Streams

Wealth creation is rarely the result of a single income source. While a steady paycheck may provide stability, true financial growth and resilience often stem from diversified income sources. By generating multiple streams of income, you not only increase your earning potential but also build a financial safety net, reducing the risk associated with dependence on a single source. This chapter will explore the different types of income streams and provide actionable insights on how to create a diversified income portfolio that aligns with your financial goals.

* * *

Why Multiple Income Streams Matter

1. Financial Security and Resilience

Relying on one income source leaves you vulnerable to economic shifts, job loss, or industry changes. Diversifying income reduces risk and creates a buffer that keeps your finances steady even if one source fluctuates.

2. Accelerated Wealth-Building

With multiple income streams, you're able to allocate more funds toward savings, investments, and other wealth-building activities. These additional resources can help you achieve financial goals faster.

3. Freedom and Flexibility

Diversified income offers freedom from traditional constraints, providing flexibility in how you work, spend, and save. This flexibility can empower you to take risks, explore passions, and create a lifestyle aligned with your values.

* * *

Types of Income Streams

Income can be classified into various types, each with unique benefits and potential. Understanding these types can help you make informed choices about where to focus your efforts.

1. Earned Income

Earned income is the most common and straightforward type: the wages or salary you receive from employment. While reliable, it often requires significant time and effort, making it difficult to scale without working longer hours or advancing into higher-paying positions.

2. Business Income

Income generated from a business you own or partially own can provide more freedom and potential for growth than traditional employment. While it involves risk and requires an investment of time and resources, a successful business can become a substantial income stream.

3. Interest Income

Earned through savings accounts, certificates of deposit, or lending platforms, interest income allows your money to work for you. While typically low-yield, it is one of the safest income streams and can provide passive earnings with minimal effort.

4. Dividend Income

Dividends are payments made by companies to shareholders as a share of profits. By investing in dividend-yielding stocks, you create a source of income that grows with each investment, often increasing over time as companies grow.

5. Rental Income

Real estate investments can generate rental income, providing a steady, predictable cash flow. While it requires an initial investment and maintenance, real estate can be a powerful source of passive income and wealth growth.

6. Capital Gains

Income from the sale of assets like stocks, bonds, real estate, or other investments is known as capital gains. This income stream is less predictable but can provide substantial returns, especially with a well-timed sale.

7. Royalties and Licensing

Royalties are earned from intellectual property such as books, music, patents, or artwork. Once created, these assets can generate ongoing income with little additional effort, making it a valuable form of passive income.

* * *

Building Your Income Portfolio

Creating multiple income streams involves strategic planning, disciplined investing, and sometimes a willingness to experiment. Here are some steps to get started:

1. Assess Your Skills and Resources

Take stock of your skills, assets, and available resources. Do you have expertise that could translate into a side business? Is there a hobby that could be monetized? Identify your strengths and consider how they can be leveraged into income streams.

2. Start with One Additional Income Stream

Begin by adding one new income stream, such as a part-time freelance job or a small investment. Starting small allows you to test the waters, develop skills, and build confidence without overwhelming yourself.

3. Reinvest Earnings

As new income streams generate revenue, reinvest a portion of these earnings to grow or diversify further. For example, dividends can be reinvested into additional stocks, or rental income can fund a second property investment.

4. Monitor and Adjust

Income streams may fluctuate over time, so it's essential to review your portfolio regularly. Make adjustments as needed, reallocating resources to the streams that are most profitable or promising while phasing out underperforming assets.

* * *

Strategies for Developing Passive Income

Passive income, which requires minimal ongoing effort, is a highly desirable form of income. While most passive income streams require initial work or investment, they provide long-term value with less ongoing time commitment.

1. Investing in Dividend Stocks
   Building a portfolio of dividend-paying stocks is a popular passive income strategy. By reinvesting dividends, you create a compounding effect that increases income over time, often with minimal involvement.

2. Real Estate Investments
   Rental properties, REITs (Real Estate Investment Trusts), and crowdfunding platforms make real estate a versatile passive income option. While property management can require some oversight, property managers or REIT investments provide alternatives for less hands-on involvement.

3. Peer-to-Peer Lending
   Lending through peer-to-peer platforms enables you to earn interest on your loans. Although this form of income carries some risk, diversifying across multiple loans can help balance the risk and increase earnings.

4. Creating Digital Products

E-books, online courses, and templates are digital products that can be created once and sold repeatedly. These assets continue to generate income with minimal ongoing work, especially when marketed effectively.

* * *

Balancing Active and Passive Income

While passive income can offer financial security with minimal time commitment, active income often remains an essential part of wealth-building. Finding a balance between active and passive income is crucial for a well-rounded financial strategy.

1. Use Active Income to Build Passive Streams

Allocate a portion of your earned income to fund passive income sources. For example, using salary income to purchase dividend stocks or real estate investments can create passive income streams that compound over time.

2. Set Passive Income Goals

Determine how much passive income you'd like to generate and set milestones to measure progress. Having clear goals can guide your investment choices and help you stay committed to building passive streams.

3. Maintain Flexibility

Financial needs and market conditions change, so it's essential to adapt your income strategy. Be open to adjusting your balance between active and passive income as opportunities and goals evolve.

* * *

Building Long-Term Financial Independence

Multiple income streams contribute to a larger goal: financial independence. When you're no longer reliant on a single paycheck, you have the freedom to pursue passions, retire early, or simply enjoy a higher level of security.

1. Focus on Sustainable Growth

Prioritize income sources that can grow or appreciate over time. For instance, reinvesting in dividend stocks or expanding real estate holdings can lead to compounding growth that sustains wealth over the long term.

2. Seek Continuous Learning and Skill Development

Income diversification is often linked to the ability to learn new skills and adapt to market trends. Whether it's investing, entrepreneurship, or digital product creation, continuous learning expands your earning potential and makes you more adaptable to economic shifts.

3. Build a Legacy
   Multiple income streams not only enhance your current financial situation but can also provide generational wealth. Establishing assets and income sources that can be passed down ensures financial security for future generations.

* * *

Embracing Financial Freedom Through Diverse Income

Diversifying income streams is a cornerstone of wealth-building and financial resilience. By embracing the principles of multiple income sources, you empower yourself to reach financial goals faster, reduce reliance on a single job, and create lasting financial freedom. This journey requires time, strategy, and dedication, but the rewards—greater security, flexibility, and independence—are worth the effort.

The Importance of Financial Literacy

E mpowering Your Wealth Journey Through Knowledge

In the pursuit of lifelong wealth, knowledge truly is power. Financial literacy—the ability to understand and make informed decisions about your finances—is a critical foundation for successful money management. Without it, even the most disciplined saver or high-income earner can struggle to grow wealth effectively. This chapter will explore the core components of financial literacy, including budgeting, saving, and investing. With these tools, you'll be equipped to make informed decisions, avoid costly mistakes, and take control of your financial future.

* * *

Why Financial Literacy Matters

1. Informed Decision-Making

Financial literacy empowers you to make choices that align with your goals. By understanding the fundamentals, such as the pros and cons of different investment vehicles or the impact of interest rates on loans, you gain the confidence to make decisions that serve your financial well-being.

2. Avoiding Debt Traps

Misunderstanding credit, loans, and interest can lead to debt spirals that are hard to escape. Financial literacy helps you recognize predatory lending practices, avoid unnecessary debt, and manage credit wisely.

3. Maximizing Savings and Investments

Knowing where to save and how to invest can significantly impact your wealth-building potential. When you understand concepts like compound interest, tax advantages, and diversification, you can make your money work harder for you.

* * *

The Basics of Budgeting: Your Financial Blueprint

Budgeting is the process of creating a plan for your money, ensuring that income is allocated to meet your needs, wants, and goals. It's a critical skill that keeps you on track financially, allowing you to live within your means while saving for the future.

1. Creating a Budget

Start with your income and list all monthly expenses, from fixed bills like rent and utilities to variable costs like groceries and entertainment. Categorize these expenses to see where your money goes and identify areas where you could cut back.

2. The 50/30/20 Rule

A popular budgeting approach, the 50/30/20 rule, allocates 50% of income to needs, 30% to wants, and 20% to savings or debt repayment. This structure ensures a balanced approach, prioritizing both immediate needs and future goals.

3. Tracking and Adjusting

Reviewing your budget regularly is essential. Monthly expenses and income can fluctuate, so tracking your spending helps you adapt, stay on target, and adjust as needed to avoid overspending.

* * *

The Importance of Saving: Building Financial Security

Saving is a cornerstone of financial security, providing a safety net for emergencies and creating capital for future investments. Financial literacy around saving involves understanding the different types of savings and when to use them.

1. Emergency Fund
   This fund is a cash reserve for unexpected expenses like medical bills, car repairs, or job loss. Aim for at least three to six months' worth of living expenses to ensure you're protected from financial setbacks.

2. Short-Term Savings
   Short-term goals, such as a vacation, home improvements, or a down payment, benefit from a dedicated savings account. High-yield savings accounts or money market funds are ideal as they offer liquidity with some interest.

3. Long-Term Savings and Retirement
   Long-term savings are typically invested to outpace inflation and grow over time. Retirement accounts like IRAs or employer-sponsored 401(k) plans provide tax advantages and compound growth, making them essential for financial independence.

* * *

Introduction to Investing: Growing Wealth Through Informed Choices

Investing allows you to increase your wealth by putting money into assets that have the potential to grow in value. Financial literacy in investing enables you to navigate risks, choose suitable investments, and avoid scams.

1. Risk and Return
Every investment comes with a level of risk. Generally, higher returns are associated with higher risk, and understanding this trade-off helps you choose investments that match your comfort level and financial goals.

2. Types of Investments
Common investment options include stocks, bonds, mutual funds, and real estate. Each has unique benefits, risk levels, and growth potential. Diversifying among these can help you manage risk and maximize returns.

3. Compounding
Compounding is the process where your investment returns generate additional returns, accelerating growth over time. This phenomenon underscores the importance of starting to invest early, as even small contributions can grow significantly through compounding.

* * *

Credit and Debt Management: Building Credit Responsibly

Credit and debt can be valuable tools when used wisely, but misman-agement can lead to financial strain. Financial literacy around credit helps you borrow responsibly and maintain a strong credit score.

1. Understanding Credit Scores
   Your credit score affects loan eligibility, interest rates, and even some job opportunities. Paying bills on time, keeping credit utilization low, and avoiding unnecessary credit applications can help you build and maintain a good score.

2. Types of Debt
   Not all debt is created equal. "Good debt" is typically tied to appreciating assets, such as a mortgage or education loan, while "bad debt" often relates to high-interest consumer debt. Recognizing the difference helps you make borrowing decisions that support wealth-building.

3. Debt Repayment Strategies
   Common repayment methods include the snowball (paying off the smallest debts first) and avalanche (paying off the highest-interest debts first) methods. Choosing the right strategy for you helps you reduce debt efficiently and improve your financial health.

* * *

Taxes and Financial Literacy

Taxes impact nearly every aspect of your finances. A solid understanding of tax basics, including tax brackets, deductions, and credits, is essential for maximizing your income and minimizing liabilities.

1. Understanding Your Tax Bracket
   Your tax bracket determines the rate at which your income is taxed. Knowing where you fall can help you make tax-efficient decisions, such as contributing to retirement accounts or adjusting withholding.

2. Deductions and Credits
   Tax deductions reduce your taxable income, while credits directly lower your tax bill. Being aware of eligible deductions and credits can significantly reduce your tax burden, allowing you to keep more of your income.

3. Tax-Advantaged Accounts
   Accounts like IRAs, HSAs, and 401(k)s offer tax benefits that support savings and investment goals. These accounts are valuable tools for building wealth, as they provide either tax-deferred or tax-free growth.

* * *

Building Financial Literacy for Lifelong Wealth

Financial literacy is not a one-time lesson but an ongoing journey. Staying informed about financial trends, tools, and strategies will empower you to make better decisions as you progress through life's financial stages.

1. Continuous Learning
The financial landscape evolves, with new investment options, tax regulations, and budgeting tools emerging regularly. Make it a habit to read financial books, follow reputable sources, and stay updated on changes.

2. Seeking Professional Advice
Financial advisors, tax professionals, and investment experts can offer personalized guidance. Building a trusted network of professionals ensures you receive accurate advice and stay on track toward your goals.

3. Teaching Financial Literacy to Others
Once you gain financial knowledge, consider sharing it with family members, friends, or your community. Teaching others helps reinforce your understanding and creates a positive impact that extends beyond personal wealth.

* * *

The Role of Financial Literacy in Wealth Building

Financial literacy is the foundation upon which sustainable wealth is built. It enables you to make informed decisions, avoid pitfalls, and maximize your financial potential. Whether it's budgeting, investing, or managing credit, each aspect of financial literacy contributes to a holistic understanding of money and wealth. Embrace this knowledge as a lifelong tool that guides you toward financial freedom, empowering you to shape a prosperous future with confidence and clarity.

Budgeting for Success

The Power of a Budget

Creating a lasting path to wealth requires a disciplined approach to managing your money. Budgeting isn't just about tracking expenses; it's about giving each dollar a purpose that aligns with your goals. A well-structured budget is like a financial roadmap, showing you where your money is going and ensuring it works for you. In this chapter, we'll explore how budgeting can become a powerful tool in building wealth and examine strategies for sticking to it, minimizing excess, and achieving long-term financial freedom.

* * *

Why Budgeting Matters

Budgeting is more than a tool—it's a mindset shift that encourages you to think critically about every dollar. Instead of spending impulsively, budgeting helps you make intentional choices that support your goals and future security.

1. Gaining Financial Clarity

A budget provides a clear snapshot of your financial health. It highlights where you're overspending and where you can save, giving you insight into how to adjust for maximum financial growth.

2. Fostering Control Over Finances

Having a budget empowers you to control your money rather than letting it control you. It enables you to set limits, prioritize essential expenses, and reduce financial stress.

3. Achieving Financial Goals

Whether saving for a major purchase, building an emergency fund, or investing, budgeting ensures you have a systematic approach to reaching your goals without falling into debt.

* * *

Building a Budget: The Fundamentals

Crafting an effective budget doesn't need to be complex. By focusing on key categories and staying organized, you can create a plan that's easy to manage and adjust as your financial situation changes.

1. Calculate Your Income

Start by identifying your monthly net income—your take-home pay after taxes and deductions. This figure will serve as the basis for all your budgeting decisions.

2. Identify Your Fixed Expenses

Fixed expenses are costs that remain the same every month, like rent, utilities, and loan payments. These expenses are essential, so they'll take priority in your budget.

3. Outline Variable Expenses

Variable expenses, such as groceries, transportation, and entertainment, fluctuate month to month. Track these expenses to see where you may be able to cut back.

4. Set Aside Savings and Investments

Prioritize saving and investing by setting aside a portion of your income for future growth. Automate this process, so you're consistently building wealth without effort.

5. Allocate for Fun and Flexibility

It's essential to include a category for hobbies, entertainment, or dining out. Budgeting for these areas prevents overspending while still allowing you to enjoy life.

* * *

Popular Budgeting Methods

Selecting a budgeting method that suits your lifestyle and goals can make managing money more approachable and enjoyable. Here are some of the most effective methods:

1. 50/30/20 Rule
   In this approach, allocate 50% of your income to needs, 30% to wants, and 20% to savings or debt repayment. This method keeps your finances balanced and focuses on building savings.

2. Zero-Based Budgeting
   Every dollar has a job in zero-based budgeting, meaning you assign each dollar to a specific purpose until you have zero remaining. This method promotes mindful spending and maximizes savings.

3. Envelope System
   The envelope system is a cash-based approach where you divide money into envelopes labeled for different spending categories. It's highly effective for those who prefer a hands-on, visual method to manage expenses.

4. Percentage-Based Budgeting
   This method involves assigning specific percentages to categories like savings, debt repayment, and discretionary spending. It allows

flexibility and can be customized to match personal priorities.

5. Priority-Based Budgeting
    This approach focuses on prioritizing essential categories over less important ones. You may allocate more towards savings, for example, if achieving financial independence is your top goal.

* * *

Tips for Sticking to Your Budget

Setting a budget is the first step, but following it consistently is where true discipline and success lie. Here are practical tips to help you stick to your budget:

1. Track Your Spending
    Use an app or notebook to track daily expenses. By keeping tabs on where your money is going, you can avoid overspending and identify areas for improvement.

2. Review Monthly
    At the end of each month, assess your spending patterns. This review helps you understand if you're staying within your budget and make adjustments for the following month.

3. Automate Bills and Savings

Automating fixed expenses and savings reduces the risk of forgetting payments and encourages consistent saving habits.

4. Create a "Miscellaneous" Category

Unexpected expenses can throw off a budget, so allocate a small portion of funds for miscellaneous costs. This category provides flexibility while keeping you on track.

5. Use Cash for Discretionary Spending

Cash limits spending on non-essential items since, once it's gone, you can't overspend. The physical act of handing over cash often makes people more mindful of their purchases.

* * *

Living Below Your Means: A Wealth-Building Strategy

Living below your means means spending less than you earn, allowing you to save and invest for the future. This practice is one of the cornerstones of wealth building.

1. Cutting Unnecessary Expenses

Identify areas where you can reduce spending, such as dining out or subscription services you rarely use. Even small adjustments can accumulate over time, freeing up funds for savings.

2. Finding Affordable Alternatives
Seek affordable options for regular purchases, whether it's cooking meals at home instead of dining out or choosing generic brands over name brands. These minor changes add up significantly.

3. Delay Gratification
Avoid impulse purchases by waiting 24 hours before buying non-essential items. This practice encourages mindful spending and reduces unnecessary expenses.

4. Avoiding Lifestyle Inflation
As income increases, it's easy to raise your standard of living. By maintaining your current lifestyle and saving the extra income, you can accelerate wealth accumulation without sacrificing comfort.

* * *

Setting Financial Goals to Support Your Budget

A budget is most effective when aligned with clear, achievable financial goals. Goal-setting provides direction and purpose, helping you stay motivated and committed.

1. Short-Term Goals

These goals, such as saving for a trip or paying off a credit card, typically span one year or less. Short-term goals provide immediate satisfaction and build momentum toward bigger achievements.

2. Medium-Term Goals

Spanning one to five years, medium-term goals may include buying a car, completing a home renovation, or building an emergency fund. They require more commitment and planning than short-term goals.

3. Long-Term Goals

Long-term goals like retirement savings or buying a home may take decades. These goals form the backbone of your wealth-building strategy, ensuring lasting financial security.

* * *

Budgeting Tools and Resources

Numerous tools can make budgeting easier, more organized, and efficient. Here are some popular options:

1. Budgeting Apps
    Apps like Mint, YNAB (You Need a Budget), and PocketGuard help you track spending, set goals, and receive insights on your financial habits.

2. Spreadsheets
    Budgeting spreadsheets, whether custom-made or downloadable templates, allow you to personalize categories and track expenses manually.

3. Banking Tools
    Many banks offer built-in budgeting tools and spending analyses that can simplify tracking expenses and setting savings goals.

4. Online Calculators
    Financial calculators for savings, debt, and investments help you estimate future growth and understand how your budget decisions impact long-term wealth.

* * *

Budgeting as the Key to Financial Freedom

Mastering your budget is a powerful step toward achieving financial independence. By thoughtfully allocating each dollar, cutting unnecessary expenses, and living below your means, you create a surplus that can be used for savings, investment, and wealth-building. Budgeting is not about restriction; it's about empowerment. As you continue on your wealth journey, let your budget be a guiding tool, providing clarity, control, and confidence in reaching your lifelong financial goals.

The Role of Saving in Wealth Building

T he Purpose of Saving

Saving isn't just about putting money aside—it's about creating a financial safety net, fueling investments, and securing long-term stability. Saving consistently is one of the most foundational steps in building wealth, yet many overlook its potential power. A structured approach to saving can transform your financial future, offering not only security but the ability to seize opportunities as they arise. In this chapter, we'll explore why saving is essential, how to approach it strategically, and ways to ensure your savings grow effectively over time.

* * *

Why Saving is Essential for Wealth

Saving serves as a cornerstone for financial security. It's the first step toward achieving major goals, protecting yourself against unforeseen expenses, and creating a pathway to financial freedom. The process of saving teaches discipline and lays the groundwork for other wealth-building activities.

1. Building Financial Security
Savings act as a buffer against life's uncertainties. An emergency fund, for example, ensures you can manage unexpected expenses without derailing your long-term plans.

2. Creating Capital for Investments
Saving consistently allows you to accumulate capital, which can be directed into investments. This capital growth is the foundation of a diversified financial portfolio.

3. Supporting Life Goals
Whether it's buying a home, funding education, or starting a business, saving allows you to work toward significant life goals without relying on debt or high-interest loans.

* * *

Types of Savings and Their Purpose

Each type of savings has a distinct role and aligns with specific financial objectives. By understanding and categorizing your savings, you can ensure you're prepared for various financial needs.

1. Emergency Fund

An emergency fund is a cash reserve meant for unforeseen expenses like medical bills, car repairs, or temporary loss of income. A well-funded emergency account reduces the need to rely on credit or withdraw from long-term investments in times of crisis.

2. Short-Term Savings

Short-term savings are for goals that you plan to achieve within a few months to a couple of years, like a vacation, a new gadget, or a down payment on a car. Keeping these funds in a high-yield savings account can offer security and accessibility while still earning interest.

3. Long-Term Savings

Long-term savings are reserved for goals that span several years, like retirement or buying a home. These funds often benefit from compounding interest over time, making it essential to start saving as early as possible.

4. Investment Capital

While technically not just savings, setting aside money specifically for investments allows you to participate in wealth-building opportunities, such as stocks, real estate, or mutual funds, without risking your core savings.

* * *

Strategies for Effective Saving

Building a savings habit requires consistency and a clear strategy. Here are methods to make saving a seamless part of your financial routine.

1. Automate Savings Contributions
   Setting up automatic transfers to your savings account removes the need to manually save money and ensures consistency. Many banks allow you to automate transfers on each payday, so you're saving without even thinking about it.

2. Pay Yourself First
   Rather than saving what's left after spending, prioritize savings by treating it as a non-negotiable "expense." This approach ensures that saving becomes a primary focus, not an afterthought.

3. Use Percentage-Based Saving
   Committing a percentage of your income, rather than a fixed amount, allows your savings contributions to grow as your earnings increase. Start with a realistic percentage—say 10%—and gradually increase it as your financial situation improves.

4. Apply the "52-Week Savings Challenge"
   This popular method encourages incremental saving by starting with a small amount, such as $1, in the first week, and increasing it by

$1 each week. By the end of the year, you'll have saved a substantial amount with minimal effort.

5. Set Clear Savings Goals

Define specific, measurable savings goals for each category (emergency, short-term, and long-term). Having a tangible goal creates motivation and makes the process more rewarding.

* * *

Avoiding Common Saving Pitfalls

While saving is crucial, several common mistakes can derail your progress. Awareness of these pitfalls can help you maintain consistency and protect your hard-earned savings.

1. Dipping into Savings Frequently

Repeatedly withdrawing from your savings undermines its purpose. To prevent this, establish a strict policy for when you're allowed to access your savings and create a "cool-off" period to assess if the expense is truly necessary.

2. Setting Unrealistic Savings Targets

Aim for achievable targets that align with your income and expenses.

Setting overly ambitious goals can lead to frustration and may tempt you to abandon the process altogether.

3. Failing to Adjust for Inflation
Over time, inflation erodes the value of cash savings. Consider keeping a portion of your long-term savings in accounts that offer competitive interest rates or exploring investments that can outpace inflation.

4. Neglecting to Reevaluate Goals
Life changes, and so should your savings goals. Regularly review and adjust your savings strategy to ensure it aligns with your current financial situation and future aspirations.

* * *

Maximizing Savings Growth: Interest and Compounding

Beyond simply saving, it's crucial to maximize the growth of your money through interest and compounding. Here's how these tools can accelerate your wealth-building journey.

1. High-Yield Savings Accounts
Look for high-yield savings accounts that offer competitive interest

rates. Although they may not grow as quickly as investments, they provide a safe, accessible way to earn more on your savings.

2. Certificates of Deposit (CDs)

CDs are fixed-term savings options that typically offer higher interest rates than regular savings accounts. By locking in your funds for a specific period, you can benefit from higher returns.

3. Take Advantage of Compounding Interest

Compounding occurs when interest earned on your savings starts generating interest itself. The earlier you start saving, the more time compounding has to work, which can result in exponential growth over time.

4. Reinvesting Earnings

When your savings earn interest, consider reinvesting the earnings back into the savings account rather than withdrawing them. This approach enhances the compounding effect, helping your savings grow faster.

* * *

Balancing Saving with Debt Repayment

While saving is essential, addressing any outstanding debt is equally important. Balancing savings and debt repayment requires a thoughtful approach that aligns with your financial priorities.

1. Prioritize High-Interest Debt

Pay off high-interest debts, such as credit card balances, before aggressively saving, as these debts often accrue interest faster than savings accounts. Once high-interest debts are managed, you can shift focus back to building savings.

2. Build a Small Emergency Fund First

Before aggressively tackling debt, set aside a small emergency fund (typically 1-3 months of expenses). This fund prevents you from incurring more debt if unexpected expenses arise.

3. Establish a Debt Repayment Plan

Outline a structured repayment plan alongside your savings goals. Allocate a portion of your income to both debt and savings, ensuring you make steady progress on both fronts.

* * *

Incorporating Saving into Your Financial Lifestyle

True wealth-building involves making saving a non-negotiable part of your lifestyle. By weaving saving habits into your everyday life, you can make financial security feel natural rather than restrictive.

1. Live Below Your Means
   Spending less than you earn frees up more money to save. Avoid lifestyle inflation, or the tendency to increase spending as income grows, to maximize your savings potential.

2. Focus on Quality over Quantity
   Practice mindful spending by investing in quality items that last longer, even if they cost more initially. This habit reduces frequent replacements, leaving more funds available for saving.

3. Celebrate Milestones
   Recognize and celebrate when you reach key savings milestones. Acknowledging your achievements provides motivation and reinforces the positive impact of your efforts.

4. Stay Inspired by Financial Success Stories
   Learning about others who have achieved financial freedom through disciplined saving can provide inspiration. Emulating their strategies and mindset can help keep you committed to your own goals.

* * *

Saving as the Backbone of Financial Independence

Saving is a fundamental component of wealth-building. It empowers you to manage life's uncertainties, create opportunities for growth, and work toward meaningful financial goals. Through disciplined saving, strategic planning, and a commitment to long-term growth, you're laying the foundation for a prosperous future. By incorporating these practices into your daily life, you're not just accumulating money; you're building financial independence, security, and freedom for the years to come.

Strategic Investing for Long-Term Growth

T he Value of Investing for Wealth

Saving money lays the foundation, but investing is the vehicle that accelerates your journey to financial prosperity. Strategic investing involves carefully selecting assets, balancing risk and reward, and exercising patience to allow compounding growth. A thoughtful, disciplined investment approach can turn modest sums into substantial wealth over time. This chapter will guide you through the essentials of investing, from understanding asset classes to managing risk, highlighting how each decision contributes to long-term wealth.

* * *

Understanding Different Asset Classes

Investing spans a wide range of assets, each with unique risk and return characteristics. Knowing the distinctions among these classes is essential for building a diversified, resilient portfolio.

1. Stocks (Equities)

Stocks represent ownership in a company. Historically, they offer high returns, especially over the long term, though they also carry volatility. Investing in stocks can be approached through individual shares or diversified via exchange-traded funds (ETFs) and mutual funds.

2. Bonds

Bonds are debt securities issued by corporations or governments, offering lower returns than stocks but greater stability. They provide predictable interest payments, making them suitable for conservative portfolios seeking steady growth.

3. Real Estate

Real estate investments include residential, commercial, and industrial properties. Real estate can offer both rental income and appreciation. While it requires a larger initial investment, it can also provide steady cash flow and potential tax benefits.

4. Commodities

Commodities like gold, oil, and agricultural products provide a hedge against inflation and currency fluctuations. These assets can be volatile but serve as diversification tools, especially when traditional markets experience downturns.

5. Cryptocurrency

Cryptocurrencies like Bitcoin and Ethereum offer high-risk, high-reward potential. This emerging asset class carries extreme volatility but has gained popularity for diversification. Understanding the technology and market dynamics is critical for crypto investments.

6. Alternative Investments

Alternative investments—such as private equity, hedge funds, and collectibles—are less liquid and often require higher capital. They can offer unique opportunities for growth and diversification outside of traditional assets.

* * *

Crafting a Diversified Portfolio

Diversification spreads risk by allocating investments across different asset classes, industries, and geographic regions. This strategy reduces the impact of poor performance in any one area, helping stabilize returns over time.

1. Asset Allocation

Asset allocation refers to the percentage of your portfolio invested in each asset class. A common model is the "60/40" portfolio (60% stocks, 40% bonds) for balanced growth and stability. Tailor your allocation to your goals and risk tolerance, adjusting as you age or as your financial situation changes.

2. Sector and Geographic Diversification

Investing in multiple sectors—like technology, healthcare, and finance—protects against market downturns in specific industries. Similarly, global investments can buffer against economic challenges within a single country.

3. Rebalancing Your Portfolio

Periodically adjusting your portfolio's allocation back to its original or target state helps maintain the intended risk level. This involves selling assets that have grown beyond their designated percentage and reinvesting in underweighted assets.

4. Dollar-Cost Averaging

This strategy involves regularly investing a fixed amount into the market, regardless of price. Dollar-cost averaging reduces the impact of market volatility, as you buy more shares when prices are low and fewer when prices are high.

* * *

Risk Management Strategies

All investments carry risk, but effective risk management can help you mitigate losses and protect your capital. These strategies ensure you're positioned to handle both market fluctuations and unexpected economic changes.

1. Know Your Risk Tolerance

Risk tolerance reflects your comfort level with losing money for potential gains. Younger investors may take on higher-risk investments due to longer time horizons, while conservative investors might prioritize stability.

2. Use Stop-Loss Orders

Stop-loss orders automatically sell a stock if its price falls to a specified level, helping limit potential losses. This tool is essential for managing risk in volatile markets and can be particularly helpful for high-risk assets.

3. Consider Hedging

Hedging involves taking offsetting positions to protect your portfolio against adverse movements. For example, owning bonds can serve as a hedge against stock market downturns, as bonds often rise when stocks fall.

4. Maintain an Emergency Fund

Before investing aggressively, build an emergency fund to cover three to six months of expenses. This fund provides security, allowing you to avoid liquidating investments in emergencies.

* * *

The Power of Compounding

Compounding occurs when your investment earnings generate additional returns over time. By reinvesting returns, you essentially earn interest on interest, allowing even small contributions to grow significantly.

1. Start Early
   The sooner you begin investing, the more time your investments have to compound. For example, an investment of $10,000 growing at 7% annually will double approximately every ten years, reaching $80,000 in four decades without additional contributions.

2. Reinvest Dividends
   Many stocks pay dividends, or a portion of earnings, to shareholders. Reinvesting dividends rather than cashing them out accelerates compounding and enhances long-term growth.

3. Consistent Contributions
   Regularly adding to your investments, even in small amounts, max-

imizes compounding benefits. Over time, consistent contributions lead to exponential growth, even if market returns vary year to year.

* * *

Investment Strategies for Different Goals

Every financial goal may require a unique investment strategy. Tailoring your approach helps you meet specific objectives, whether they are short-term, mid-term, or long-term.

1. Short-Term Goals (1–3 Years)
   For goals with a short timeline, prioritize capital preservation. Consider low-risk options like high-yield savings accounts, certificates of deposit, or short-term bonds that offer stability over growth.

2. Medium-Term Goals (3–10 Years)
   For goals in the medium range, like a down payment on a home, consider balanced portfolios with a mix of stocks, bonds, and ETFs. These investments offer moderate growth while mitigating high risk.

3. Long-Term Goals (10+ Years)
   Retirement or legacy-building goals often benefit from a high allocation to stocks and growth-oriented assets. These provide the

potential for significant appreciation over time, and the long horizon helps weather market volatility.

4. Tax-Advantaged Accounts

Maximize contributions to tax-advantaged accounts, such as IRAs and 401(k)s. These accounts offer tax benefits, either in the form of immediate deductions or tax-free growth, helping your investments grow faster.

* * *

The Importance of Patience and Discipline

Investing isn't about quick profits; it's a marathon that requires patience, discipline, and a long-term view. Financial markets fluctuate, but a disciplined approach helps navigate both highs and lows.

1. Avoid Market Timing

Trying to "time the market"—or buying and selling based on short-term trends—is notoriously difficult and can lead to costly mistakes. A buy-and-hold strategy, where you invest consistently and hold assets for the long term, generally yields better results.

2. Stay Informed, But Avoid Overreacting

Follow market news and trends to remain aware of shifts that may affect your investments. However, avoid making hasty decisions based on short-term market movements or news events, which can lead to emotional investing.

3. Review Progress Annually
Set aside time each year to review your portfolio's performance and adjust your allocation if needed. This annual check-in ensures your investments stay aligned with your goals and that you're adapting to life changes.

* * *

Common Mistakes to Avoid

Even the most experienced investors make mistakes, but learning about common pitfalls can help you avoid them and stay on course toward your financial goals.

1. Chasing Hot Stocks
Popular stocks can seem attractive, but investing based on hype often leads to disappointment. Instead, focus on companies with strong fundamentals and a history of growth.

2. Overtrading

Frequent buying and selling can incur high fees and tax liabilities. Stick to your strategy and avoid overtrading, which erodes returns and increases risk.

3. Ignoring Fees

Investment fees, including fund management fees and brokerage commissions, can significantly impact your returns over time. Choose low-cost investments and review fee structures before committing.

* * *

Investing as a Path to Prosperity

Investing strategically creates a pathway to wealth that grows steadily over time. By diversifying your portfolio, managing risk, and exercising patience, you're building a resilient financial future. Your investments become more than just numbers—they represent your commitment to a prosperous life, one that is financially secure and filled with opportunities. As you continue refining your investment strategy, remember that wealth is built on a series of smart, consistent choices. Stay committed, keep learning, and embrace the journey toward lifelong prosperity.

Real Estate as a Wealth-Building Tool

The Potential of Real Estate for Financial Growth

Real estate has long been regarded as a cornerstone of wealth-building strategies. Unlike other investments, real estate offers tangible assets with potential for steady appreciation, cash flow, and multiple financial benefits. Whether through rental income, property appreciation, or equity building, real estate provides a multifaceted approach to growing wealth. In this chapter, we'll dive into the fundamentals of real estate investing, including how to leverage properties, build equity, and generate passive income.

* * *

Why Real Estate is a Unique Asset Class

Real estate stands apart from other asset classes for its stability, tangible value, and ability to serve multiple purposes. This section explores the unique benefits of real estate and its potential to secure long-term financial growth.

1. Tangible and Finite Asset

Unlike stocks or digital assets, real estate represents physical property that serves practical needs, such as housing or commercial space. Its finite nature often leads to appreciation, as demand for space increases with population growth and economic expansion.

2. Less Volatile Than Equities

Real estate typically experiences less volatility than stocks, offering a buffer against market downturns. This stability is especially beneficial for investors seeking steady growth with minimal fluctuations.

3. Dual Revenue Streams

Properties can provide two forms of returns: regular income through rent and capital gains through appreciation. This dual approach supports both short-term cash flow and long-term growth.

4. Tax Advantages

Real estate investment comes with significant tax benefits, including deductions for mortgage interest, property taxes, depreciation, and repair costs. For investors, these deductions reduce taxable income, increasing overall returns.

* * *

Investing in Rental Properties

Rental properties are one of the most popular methods for generating passive income and building equity. From single-family homes to multi-unit complexes, rental properties can offer reliable cash flow when managed effectively.

1. Choosing the Right Location

Location is crucial in real estate. Properties in growing areas with low crime rates, good schools, and robust job markets tend to attract tenants and appreciate in value. Analyze neighborhood trends, economic growth, and proximity to amenities before investing.

2. Calculating Cash Flow and ROI

Cash flow is the income generated from rent after expenses, such as mortgage payments, taxes, insurance, and maintenance. Calculating the return on investment (ROI) helps determine a property's profitability. A solid ROI benchmark for rental properties is typically around 8-12%, though this may vary based on market conditions.

3. Property Management Considerations

Managing a property requires time and resources. Decide whether to handle tasks like tenant screening, maintenance, and rent collection yourself or hire a property manager. Professional managers typically charge a percentage of the monthly rent, but they offer expertise and save time.

4. Mitigating Risks with Insurance

Protecting your property through comprehensive insurance is essential. Landlord insurance covers property damage, liability, and potential loss of rental income in case of unforeseen events. Additionally, requiring tenants to carry renter's insurance helps reduce liability risks.

* * *

Leveraging Equity for Wealth Growth

Building equity in a property over time provides an asset that can be tapped into for future investments. Leveraging this equity through refinancing or home equity loans allows you to reinvest and scale your real estate portfolio.

1. Understanding Equity

Equity is the difference between the property's market value and the amount owed on the mortgage. As the property appreciates and the mortgage balance decreases, your equity grows, creating a valuable asset.

2. Cash-Out Refinancing

Cash-out refinancing replaces your current mortgage with a larger one, providing cash based on the equity in your property. This cash can be reinvested in additional properties, renovations, or other wealth-building opportunities.

3. Home Equity Line of Credit (HELOC)

A HELOC allows you to borrow against your property's equity as a revolving line of credit. This flexibility is ideal for covering short-term expenses or financing property improvements, enhancing the property's value and rental potential.

4. Risks of Over-Leveraging

While leveraging equity can accelerate portfolio growth, over-leveraging increases financial risk. Carefully evaluate debt levels and ensure cash flow from rental income is sufficient to cover mortgage payments and other expenses.

* * *

Real Estate Investment Trusts (REITs): A Passive Approach

For those seeking real estate exposure without the responsibility of direct ownership, Real Estate Investment Trusts (REITs) offer an alternative. REITs are companies that own, operate, or finance income-generating properties and distribute a large portion of their profits as dividends to investors.

1. Types of REITs

REITs come in various forms, including equity REITs (owning property), mortgage REITs (providing financing), and hybrid REITs (a combination of both). Equity REITs typically focus on long-term property appreciation, while mortgage REITs generate income from interest on mortgages.

2. Benefits of REITs

REITs provide liquidity, diversification, and dividend income, making them an appealing option for investors who want real estate exposure without direct property management. They also offer diversification across property types, such as commercial, residential, and industrial.

3. Evaluating REIT Performance

When investing in REITs, evaluate factors like dividend yield, payout ratio, and portfolio diversity. Strong REITs consistently generate rental income, maintain low vacancy rates, and manage properties in growing regions.

* * *

House Hacking: An Entry-Level Strategy

House hacking involves living in a property while renting out part of it, such as a multi-unit property or spare rooms. This strategy allows you to offset your mortgage with rental income, reducing living costs and building equity simultaneously.

1. Selecting the Right Property
Multi-family properties, such as duplexes or triplexes, are ideal for house hacking, as they allow you to rent out separate units. Ensure the property is in a desirable location, with features that attract tenants.

2. Financing Options for House Hacking
Many house hackers use FHA loans, which require a lower down payment and offer more flexible approval criteria. These loans are ideal for first-time buyers and require that you live in one of the units, making it easier to qualify.

3. Calculating Expenses and Cash Flow
Calculate rental income against expenses, including mortgage payments, property taxes, and maintenance. Effective house hacking should cover or reduce your monthly housing costs, making it easier to save and invest elsewhere.

4. Transitioning to Full Rental Income
After building equity, some house hackers move out and rent the entire property. This transition allows them to retain the asset while generating full rental income, contributing further to their wealth-building journey.

* * *

The Role of Market Cycles in Real Estate

Understanding real estate market cycles can help you make better investment decisions, knowing when to buy, hold, or sell properties based on economic conditions and demand.

1. Phases of the Real Estate Cycle
   The real estate cycle typically includes recovery, expansion, hyper-supply, and recession phases. Each phase offers unique opportunities, with expansion phases often seeing price increases and higher demand, while recession phases present potential buying opportunities.

2. Strategies for Different Market Phases
   During expansion, consider purchasing properties as prices rise, generating higher cash flows. In recession phases, focus on acquiring undervalued assets or refinancing properties at lower interest rates.

3. Timing and Patience in Real Estate
   Real estate investing requires patience, as properties take time to appreciate and cycles can last several years. Avoid making impulsive decisions based on short-term trends, and focus on the long-term potential of your investment.

* * *

Real Estate as a Pillar of Wealth Creation

Real estate remains a powerful wealth-building tool, offering the potential for passive income, appreciation, and diversification. By understanding the different types of real estate investments, mastering financing strategies, and leveraging equity, you can create a resilient portfolio that grows steadily over time. Real estate is a tangible asset that serves both immediate and long-term goals, supporting a stable and prosperous financial future. As you continue on your path to prosperity, remember that real estate isn't just about properties; it's about making intentional, informed decisions that lead to enduring wealth.

Developing Passive Income Streams

The Power of Passive Income in Achieving Financial Independence

Passive income has become one of the most sought-after strategies for attaining financial freedom. Unlike active income, which requires continuous effort and time, passive income sources work independently, generating revenue with minimal intervention. This chapter delves into the various ways to create and sustain passive income, enabling you to build wealth efficiently and free up time for pursuits that align with your personal goals.

* * *

Understanding Passive Income: What Sets It Apart?

Passive income is distinct in its potential to generate consistent returns without constant input. While it requires an initial investment of time, money, or expertise, the rewards accumulate with minimal day-to-day involvement. This section outlines the key benefits of passive income and why it should be a foundational component of any wealth-building plan.

1. Freedom and Flexibility

Passive income grants the freedom to pursue other opportunities, whether personal or professional, while your income sources generate returns. This flexibility creates financial security, reducing reliance on a single paycheck.

2. Compounding Growth

Many passive income streams, especially those involving investments, benefit from compounding. Over time, your earnings reinvest, generating additional income, which accelerates growth.

3. Stability in Financial Planning

Passive income streams provide stability, as they often function independently of external economic or market conditions. Having multiple streams also reduces the financial risks associated with relying on a single income source.

* * *

Types of Passive Income Streams

Creating passive income involves diversifying your portfolio across different types of income streams, each with unique requirements and benefits. Here's an overview of some popular passive income sources, covering both traditional and modern approaches.

1. Dividend Stocks

Investing in dividend-paying stocks is a time-tested method of generating passive income. Dividends are regular payments made by companies to their shareholders, usually from profits. Selecting stocks from well-established companies with a history of stable or increasing dividends can provide reliable income.

Steps to Get Started: Research companies with solid dividend yields, open a brokerage account, and set up a dividend reinvestment plan (DRIP) to benefit from compounding growth.

2. Real Estate Rentals

Real estate can generate passive income through rental properties, where tenants' payments cover the mortgage and expenses, creating profit over time. Real estate rentals range from long-term residential properties to short-term vacation rentals, each with varying management requirements.

Getting Started: Choose properties in high-demand locations, secure favorable financing, and consider hiring a property manager for hands-off management.

3. Peer-to-Peer Lending

Peer-to-peer (P2P) lending platforms allow you to lend money to individuals or businesses, earning interest in return. While P2P lending carries some risk, it can generate attractive returns with the right risk management strategies.

How to Begin: Sign up on a trusted P2P platform, evaluate borrowers' creditworthiness, and diversify loans to reduce potential defaults.

4. Digital Products

Selling digital products, such as eBooks, courses, or templates, is a popular way to create passive income online. These products require upfront time and effort to develop but can be sold repeatedly with little ongoing maintenance.

Getting Started: Identify your niche, create high-quality content, and use platforms like Amazon, Udemy, or Etsy to market and sell your products.

5. Affiliate Marketing

Affiliate marketing involves promoting products or services and earning a commission on each sale made through your referral. This method requires initial work in setting up content, such as blogs or social media posts, but it can generate income with little ongoing effort.

How to Start: Select affiliate programs that align with your interests, create valuable content, and promote links through websites, social media, or email marketing.

6. Royalties from Intellectual Property

For creatives, royalties from intellectual property—such as books, music, photography, or patents—offer a means of generating passive income. These assets can be licensed or sold, earning royalties over time without continuous work.

Getting Started: Develop high-quality creative work, register for copyright protection if needed, and license or distribute through reputable platforms.

* * *

Establishing Sustainable Passive Income

Building sustainable passive income streams requires initial effort, planning, and, often, some upfront investment. To maximize returns, consider the following strategies:

1. Automate Wherever Possible

Automation tools reduce the time and effort needed to manage passive income streams. For example, automated investing apps or scheduling tools can streamline processes, making passive income truly hands-off.

2. Diversify Your Passive Income Sources

Just as with any investment, diversification is essential in passive income. Relying on a single stream can lead to risk if that income source becomes unstable. Diversify across different areas—stocks, real estate, digital products, and more—to create a more resilient portfolio.

3. Monitor and Adjust Periodically

While passive income should require minimal effort, periodic reviews are essential. Track performance, assess any risks, and make adjustments as necessary to sustain and grow each income stream over time.

* * *

Case Study: Building Multiple Income Streams

Consider Sarah, a professional who began building passive income streams with a modest investment in dividend stocks. Over time, she added rental properties, a digital course, and an affiliate marketing website. Her strategy involved reinvesting profits from one stream into another, allowing her portfolio to grow exponentially. Today, Sarah enjoys financial independence, with her passive income covering her monthly expenses, allowing her the flexibility to pursue new interests.

* * *

Common Pitfalls in Passive Income Development

While passive income holds great promise, it's essential to avoid common mistakes that can limit success or lead to setbacks.

1. Neglecting Due Diligence
   Whether investing in stocks or P2P lending, conducting thorough research and due diligence is critical. Neglecting this can lead to poor choices and financial losses.

2. Overlooking Initial Time and Money Investment
   Some passive income strategies, such as real estate or digital product creation, require substantial upfront investments. Plan accordingly and avoid overextending financially to avoid potential burnout or financial stress.

3. Expecting Immediate Results
   Passive income streams often take time to establish and yield significant returns. Patience and consistent effort in the early stages are essential for long-term success.

* * *

The Road to Financial Freedom through Passive Income

Creating passive income streams is a key component of financial independence and wealth building. By diversifying income sources, automating processes, and continually reinvesting returns, you can establish a steady financial foundation that grows with minimal ongoing effort. As you cultivate these income streams, remember that each represents a step toward freedom—allowing you to shape your life and priorities with greater control.

Leveraging Debt for Investment Opportunities

Rethinking Debt as a Tool for Wealth

Debt often has a negative connotation, associated with financial strain and poor money management. However, when used strategically, debt can become a powerful instrument in building wealth. By borrowing funds to invest in income-generating assets, you can amplify your earning potential and achieve financial goals faster. This chapter explores the concept of "good debt" versus "bad debt," highlighting how responsible leverage can maximize your investment returns.

* * *

Understanding Good Debt vs. Bad Debt

1. Good Debt

Good debt refers to borrowed funds used for investments or assets that have the potential to generate value or income over time. Examples include real estate loans, student loans for career-advancing education, and business loans. When managed carefully, good debt can yield returns that outpace the cost of borrowing.

2. Bad Debt

Bad debt, on the other hand, typically involves borrowing for consumable items or assets that depreciate, such as credit card debt for lifestyle purchases. This type of debt rarely contributes to long-term financial growth and often comes with high interest rates.

* * *

The Benefits of Leveraging Debt for Investments

1. Accelerated Wealth Growth

Borrowing money for income-producing investments, like real estate or stocks, allows you to amplify your returns without waiting to save the entire amount. For example, a mortgage on a rental property enables you to earn rental income while building property equity over time.

2. Increased Purchasing Power

By using leverage, you can invest in larger or more diverse assets than would be possible with just your savings. For instance, leveraging a down payment into a mortgage enables access to real estate with a fraction of the full property cost.

3. Tax Advantages

Interest on certain types of debt, such as mortgages and business loans, may be tax-deductible. This benefit reduces the effective cost of borrowing, enhancing the financial viability of leveraging debt for investments.

* * *

Strategies for Leveraging Debt Responsibly

1. Start with a Strong Credit Score

Your credit score affects the interest rates and loan terms you're offered, influencing your overall borrowing costs. A high credit score can make debt cheaper and more manageable, so it's wise to maintain good credit before taking on investment-related debt.

2. Calculate Potential ROI Carefully

Before borrowing to invest, it's crucial to ensure that your expected return on investment (ROI) exceeds the cost of debt. Use conservative estimates to account for any market fluctuations, ensuring the investment will remain viable even under less favorable conditions.

3. Set Clear Boundaries on Borrowing Limits

Resist the temptation to over-leverage. Establish limits on the percentage of your portfolio that is financed with debt, aiming to keep overall risk manageable and avoid undue financial strain.

4. Maintain an Emergency Fund

Leveraged investments carry an element of risk, as borrowed funds come with repayment obligations regardless of your investment's performance. Having an emergency fund provides a safety net, ensuring you can meet debt obligations in case of unexpected setbacks.

* * *

Types of Debt for Investment Opportunities

1. Mortgages for Real Estate Investment

Mortgages are one of the most popular forms of leverage for real estate investment. By financing rental or commercial properties, you can earn rental income, take advantage of property appreciation, and increase equity while repaying the loan.

2. Margin Loans for Stock Investments

Margin loans allow you to borrow against your brokerage account to purchase more stocks. This approach can amplify gains when the market rises, but it's also high-risk since losses are magnified during downturns.

3. Business Loans for Entrepreneurial Ventures

For those looking to start or expand a business, loans offer capital to grow operations, purchase equipment, or hire staff. When managed responsibly, business loans can enhance cash flow and profitability.

4. Home Equity Loans or Lines of Credit

Homeowners with equity in their property can tap into home equity loans or lines of credit to fund additional investments, such as home improvements or other income-producing ventures. Since these loans are backed by your home, they typically come with lower interest rates.

* * *

Case Study: Using Leverage to Grow a Real Estate Portfolio

Consider Alex, who started with a modest sum saved for a down payment on a rental property. By leveraging a mortgage, Alex could purchase a property worth significantly more than his savings alone would allow. Over time, rental income covered the mortgage, and property appreciation increased his equity. With the growing value of the property, Alex used a cash-out refinance to access additional funds for purchasing a second rental property. This approach allowed him to expand his real estate portfolio and build wealth much faster than saving alone.

* * *

Risks and Challenges of Leveraging Debt

1. Market Volatility
Leveraged investments can be risky in volatile markets. For instance, in a declining real estate market, property values might drop below the loan amount, making it challenging to sell or refinance.

2. Interest Rate Fluctuations
For variable-rate debt, changes in interest rates can affect loan costs and potentially strain cash flow. It's essential to consider the impact of rising interest rates on your investments.

3. Repayment Obligations
Debt must be repaid regardless of your investment performance. Failing to meet these obligations can lead to financial strain or, in severe cases, asset loss.

* * *

Best Practices for Managing Leverage

1. Monitor Debt Ratios
Keep a close eye on your debt-to-equity and loan-to-value ratios. This practice helps you avoid becoming over-leveraged, reducing financial risk.

2. Use Fixed-Rate Loans for Stability
Fixed-rate loans provide predictability, allowing you to budget for consistent payments over the life of the loan. This approach is beneficial for long-term investments where stability is essential.

3. Set Up a Debt Repayment Plan
Ensure you have a clear plan for repaying debt on time. This might include reinvesting a portion of returns toward debt reduction or setting up a sinking fund dedicated to future repayments.

* * *

Harnessing Debt Wisely to Propel Wealth Growth

Debt, when used strategically, can be a powerful asset in building wealth. By carefully selecting investment opportunities, managing debt levels, and assessing potential risks, you can use leverage to amplify your returns and accelerate financial growth. The key lies in responsible borrowing and a clear repayment strategy, ensuring that debt remains a tool for opportunity rather than a source of financial strain.

The Power of Compound Interest

U nlocking the Magic of Compound Interest

When it comes to wealth-building, compound interest stands out as one of the most potent forces at work. Albert Einstein famously referred to it as the "eighth wonder of the world." It's not just a financial concept but a strategy that, when harnessed correctly, can accelerate wealth creation and transform small, consistent investments into substantial financial growth over time. This chapter delves into the mechanics of compound interest, showing you how to leverage it to your advantage.

* * *

Understanding Compound Interest

At its core, compound interest is the interest earned on both the initial principal and the accumulated interest from previous periods. Unlike simple interest, which is calculated only on the principal amount, compound interest allows you to earn interest on your interest, creating exponential growth over time.

For example, if you invest $1,000 at an interest rate of 5%, you would earn $50 in interest the first year. The next year, however, you will earn 5% on $1,050, not just the initial $1,000, meaning your interest grows faster over time.

* * *

How Compound Interest Works

1. Principal
The initial amount of money you invest or deposit into an account. This is the base upon which interest will be calculated.

2. Interest Rate
The percentage at which your investment grows annually. The higher the interest rate, the faster your investment will grow due to the compounding effect.

3. Compounding Frequency
This refers to how often interest is added to the principal—whether daily, monthly, quarterly, or annually. The more frequently interest compounds, the greater the potential for wealth accumulation.

4. Time

Time is the most significant factor in compounding. The longer your money has to compound, the more substantial the growth, demonstrating why early investing is so powerful.

* * *

The Formula for Compound Interest

To see just how powerful compound interest can be, you can use the following formula:

$$A = P(1 + \frac{r}{n})^{nt}$$

Where:

A = the future value of the investment/loan, including interest

P = the principal investment amount (initial deposit or loan amount)

r = the annual interest rate (decimal)

n = the number of times that interest is compounded per year

t = the number of years the money is invested or borrowed for

* * *

Real-World Examples of Compound Interest

1. Early Investments: The Power of Starting Early

Let's say you invest $5,000 at a 6% annual return, compounded annually. If you let it sit for 30 years without contributing additional funds, your investment would grow to approximately $28,000. However, had you started investing just 10 years earlier, at the same rate, your investment would grow to around $89,000—an enormous difference made simply by starting earlier.

2. Reinvestment of Earnings

Another example can be seen in dividend reinvestment. Suppose you invest in dividend-paying stocks. Instead of cashing out your dividends, you reinvest them to buy more shares. Over time, those reinvested dividends begin to earn dividends themselves, leading to a snowball effect of growth.

* * *

The Impact of Time on Compound Interest

Time is the secret ingredient to the success of compound interest.

The longer your money is allowed to grow, the more pronounced the effects of compounding will be. This is why starting to save and invest as early as possible is vital for long-term wealth accumulation.

Here's an illustration:
  If you invest $1,000 at 8% annual interest:

After 10 years, you will have $2,158.92

After 20 years, you will have $4,661.88

After 30 years, you will have $10,062.65

Notice how the growth accelerates as time increases.

* * *

The Importance of Consistency

While starting early is crucial, consistency is equally important. Regularly contributing to your investment, even in small amounts, can significantly increase the total growth over time. The more frequently you invest or add funds, the more compound interest works in your favor.

For instance, if you add $100 to your account every month, the value of your investment grows much faster than if you were to deposit a lump sum once a year. This strategy allows you to take full advantage of compounding, even if you start with a smaller amount.

* * *

Why Compound Interest Is So Effective

1. Exponential Growth

Unlike simple interest, where growth is linear, compound interest grows exponentially. This exponential increase leads to larger gains over time, particularly in long-term investments like retirement funds or long-term stock investments.

2. Small Efforts, Big Rewards

The beauty of compound interest is that you don't need to make huge contributions for it to work. Even small, consistent investments will grow significantly over time, allowing you to build wealth gradually and without sacrificing current living standards.

3. Passive Wealth Creation

Once your investments are set up and earning interest, your money begins to work for you passively. You don't need to be actively managing every aspect of your investment to see returns, which frees up your time and energy for other pursuits.

* * *

Risks and Considerations in Compound Interest

1. Inflation

One risk of compounding is inflation. If your investments don't outpace inflation, your returns might not have as significant an impact on your purchasing power. This is why it's important to consider high-yield investment options, such as stocks or real estate, which tend to outgrow inflation over time.

2. Risk of Loss

Like all investments, compounding comes with the risk of loss, especially in volatile markets like stocks. It's essential to balance your portfolio and invest in diversified assets to minimize risks.

* * *

Best Practices for Maximizing Compound Interest

1. Start Early

The earlier you start investing, the more time your money has to grow exponentially through compound interest. Make investing a habit, even if it's a small amount at first.

2. Reinvest Earnings

Always reinvest the interest or dividends your investments generate to maximize the compounding effect. This builds wealth faster and helps you stay on track to meet your financial goals.

3. Be Patient

Compound interest requires time to show its true potential. Stay consistent, and be patient with your investments. The results will be worth the wait.

* * *

The Exponential Power of Compounding

Compound interest is a cornerstone of wealth-building. By understanding its mechanics and using it strategically, you can grow your wealth exponentially. The key is to start early, stay consistent, and allow time for your investments to compound. While it may seem like a slow process at first, over time, compound interest will transform small contributions into large sums, helping you achieve long-term financial prosperity. The magic of compounding lies not just in how it works, but in the patience and strategy required to harness its full potential.

Overcoming Financial Setbacks

E mbracing Resilience on the Journey to Wealth

Building wealth is rarely a smooth, uninterrupted journey. Financial setbacks are inevitable, and they can take many forms: job loss, poor investments, unexpected medical expenses, or even economic downturns. However, the difference between those who achieve lasting prosperity and those who falter lies in how they respond to these setbacks. Resilience, a mindset that embraces challenges as opportunities for growth, is key to overcoming financial difficulties and continuing forward on the path to wealth. In this chapter, we'll explore how to handle financial setbacks effectively, recover quickly, and continue your journey toward financial freedom.

* * *

Understanding Financial Setbacks

Before we can overcome financial setbacks, we need to understand what they are. Setbacks are not failures but temporary roadblocks that offer valuable lessons. These obstacles can be triggered by external events, such as market crashes, or personal mistakes, like overextending yourself financially or investing in a high-risk venture without sufficient research.

Whatever the cause, the key is not to view setbacks as permanent obstacles but as learning experiences. Adopting this perspective can help you recover faster and continue progressing toward your financial goals.

* * *

The Emotional Impact of Financial Setbacks

The emotional toll of financial setbacks can be significant. Stress, frustration, disappointment, and even fear of failure can all accompany a financial loss or crisis. It's important to recognize these emotions but not let them control your actions. Emotional reactions can cloud judgment, leading to poor decision-making, which only exacerbates the problem.

The first step in overcoming financial setbacks is emotional control. Understand that setbacks happen to everyone, and while they may be painful in the short term, they are not the end of your financial journey. Resilience is cultivated through maintaining a positive outlook and taking proactive steps, even in the face of adversity.

* * *

Step 1: Assess the Situation Objectively

The first and most important step after a financial setback is to assess the situation objectively. Take a moment to understand the full extent of the damage and what caused it. Did you overextend yourself financially? Did an investment perform poorly due to market conditions? Understanding the cause helps you avoid repeating the same mistake and enables you to formulate a plan for recovery.

Create a detailed account of your current financial position. This should include:

Current income

Outstanding debts

Savings and investments

Monthly expenses

This step allows you to take stock of your financial health and see where improvements are needed. It's crucial to have clarity on your finances before moving forward, as this will guide your recovery plan.

* * *

Step 2: Adjust Your Mindset for Recovery

The right mindset can transform a financial setback from a devastating event to a temporary challenge. Instead of focusing on the loss or disappointment, shift your focus to solutions. Ask yourself:

What can I learn from this situation?

What steps can I take to recover?

How can I improve my financial habits moving forward?

Resilience is not just about bouncing back; it's about bouncing forward with new wisdom and greater strength. Financial setbacks often provide lessons that can propel you toward smarter financial decisions in the future.

* * *

Step 3: Prioritize Immediate Financial Recovery

When faced with a financial setback, it's important to act swiftly. While long-term recovery is important, addressing short-term issues is critical. Start by stabilizing your finances. This may involve cutting unnecessary expenses, reducing debt, or liquidating non-essential assets.

Here are some immediate recovery strategies:

Create an emergency budget: Focus on essential spending, eliminating luxuries until you have regained control of your financial situation.

Negotiate with creditors: If you have outstanding debts, contact creditors to negotiate more favorable terms. This may include payment deferrals, reduced interest rates, or restructured repayment schedules.

Sell non-essential assets: If you have valuable possessions or investments that aren't core to your long-term financial strategy, consider selling them to help pay off debt or bolster your savings.

By taking immediate action, you can prevent a setback from snowballing into a long-term financial crisis.

* * *

Step 4: Build a Safety Net for Future Setbacks

One of the best ways to protect yourself from future setbacks is by building a financial safety net. Having an emergency fund is a crucial step in this process. An emergency fund provides a cushion for unexpected expenses, ensuring that you can weather financial storms without resorting to credit cards or loans.

Ideally, your emergency fund should cover three to six months of living expenses. By gradually saving this amount, you'll create a safety net that allows you to focus on long-term goals without the constant fear of financial disaster.

* * *

Step 5: Learn from Your Mistakes

Every setback, no matter how painful, provides valuable lessons. The key is to learn from them so that you don't repeat the same mistakes. Ask yourself what went wrong and how you can improve. Did you take on too much debt? Did you make investment decisions based on emotion rather than sound research? Did you neglect proper budgeting?

Use these experiences as stepping stones for improvement. The more you learn, the less likely you are to encounter the same issues in the future. Additionally, learning from mistakes helps you build a stronger financial foundation, making it easier to recover from any setbacks that may arise.

* * *

Step 6: Focus on Long-Term Goals and Persistence

While setbacks can be discouraging, it's important to maintain a long-term perspective. Wealth-building is not a race, but rather a marathon. Setbacks are part of the process, and it's the persistence to keep moving forward despite these challenges that ultimately leads to success.

Revisit your financial goals regularly. Ensure they are still in line with your long-term aspirations, and adjust them if necessary. Break these goals down into manageable steps, allowing you to track progress and celebrate small victories along the way.

Resilience is built through continued effort, even in the face of adversity. By focusing on your long-term vision, you remain motivated to push forward, no matter the challenges that may arise.

* * *

Step 7: Seek Professional Guidance

If you find that your financial setbacks are beyond your ability to recover from alone, don't hesitate to seek help from a financial advisor or coach. A professional can provide valuable insights, help you develop a recovery plan, and guide you through complex financial decisions. Sometimes, having an experienced mentor or advisor by your side can make all the difference in your recovery process.

* * *

Moving Forward with Confidence

Financial setbacks are a natural part of any wealth-building journey. What sets successful individuals apart is their ability to overcome these challenges with resilience, patience, and a growth mindset. By assessing your situation objectively, adjusting your mindset, and taking strategic action, you can recover and emerge stronger than before.

Remember, the path to prosperity is not a straight line but a series of twists and turns. Embrace setbacks as opportunities to learn and grow. Each challenge you face and overcome strengthens your financial foundation, moving you closer to the financial freedom you seek. Stay resilient, stay focused, and keep building your wealth—one step at a time.

Creating a Wealth Mindset for Business Success

The Mindset Behind Entrepreneurial Prosperity

Success in business goes beyond having the right skills or strategies; it's deeply rooted in the mindset of the entrepreneur. A wealth-focused mindset is the key to unlocking lasting business success, especially when your goal is not only to create a profitable business but to build lasting wealth. This mindset shapes how you approach challenges, manage resources, and scale your operations. In this chapter, we will explore how entrepreneurs can develop and nurture a wealth-oriented mindset that fosters sustainable business growth and long-term prosperity.

* * *

The Role of Mindset in Business

The way you think about money, growth, and opportunity profoundly impacts your business decisions. Entrepreneurs with a wealth mindset see challenges as opportunities to grow, believe in their ability to create value, and focus on long-term goals instead of short-term profits. They understand that wealth-building in business is a gradual process, requiring vision, patience, and resilience.

A business built on a wealth mindset thrives on creating value for its customers, fostering innovation, and establishing sustainable revenue streams. This mindset is not merely about making money—it's about creating a legacy of prosperity and success that can continue to grow and expand.

*　*　*

Step 1: Cultivate a Vision for Long-Term Success

A wealth mindset begins with a compelling vision. Entrepreneurs with a wealth mindset don't just focus on today's profits; they think about where their business will be in five, ten, or twenty years. A clear vision helps guide decisions, inspires action, and provides a sense of direction.

This vision should be grounded in both the entrepreneur's personal goals and the needs of the market. It's essential to continuously revisit and refine this vision to keep it aligned with the changing business environment and your own growth as an entrepreneur.

When crafting your business vision:

Define what long-term success looks like to you—financial freedom, the ability to make an impact, or creating generational wealth.

Consider how your business can evolve over time, diversifying into new markets or developing innovative products and services.

Reflect on the legacy you want to leave and the values that will guide your business practices.

A business driven by a clear and compelling vision is one that can weather economic fluctuations and build wealth over time.

* * *

Step 2: Focus on Value Creation, Not Just Profit

While profit is important, a wealth-oriented entrepreneur places greater emphasis on creating value. The most successful businesses are those that identify a market need, address it creatively, and deliver outstanding products or services. This focus on value leads to satisfied customers, repeat business, and word-of-mouth referrals, all of which contribute to long-term wealth.

To create value:

Understand your target market's pain points and desires. Listen to customer feedback, conduct surveys, and stay engaged with your audience.

Focus on innovation. Continuously seek ways to improve your product, service, or business process.

Build strong relationships with your customers, suppliers, and partners. These relationships can create opportunities for growth and collaboration.

By focusing on value, you not only build a business that generates wealth, but you also establish a reputation for excellence that can lead to enduring success.

* * *

Step 3: Embrace Smart Financial Management

Financial discipline is a hallmark of a wealth-focused mindset. Successful entrepreneurs know how to manage money wisely, ensuring that the business has enough capital to grow while also maintaining profitability. This involves creating a solid financial foundation, understanding cash flow, and investing wisely in both short-term and long-term growth.

Here are key financial management practices for wealth-building:

Create and stick to a budget: Monitor income, expenses, and profits to ensure the business remains financially sound.

Maintain healthy cash flow: Cash flow is the lifeblood of any business. Be mindful of both your inflows and outflows to avoid cash shortages.

Invest in growth: Reinvest profits into the business to fund expansion, research and development, marketing, or hiring key talent.

A business with solid financial management will be able to weather market volatility, fund growth opportunities, and provide the entrepreneur with the resources needed to build long-term wealth.

* * *

Step 4: Scale with Purpose

Scaling a business involves much more than simply increasing revenue. Entrepreneurs with a wealth mindset scale with purpose, ensuring that their growth is sustainable and aligned with their vision. They don't rush into expansion without considering the long-term implications.

When scaling a business:

Focus on profitability, not just revenue: It's easy to get caught up in chasing high sales numbers, but true wealth is built on profitability and efficiency.

Build systems and processes: As your business grows, it's essential to create scalable systems that allow for smooth operations without increasing costs disproportionately.

Diversify revenue streams: Explore new markets, products, or services to protect your business from market fluctuations and broaden its income sources.

Scaling with purpose ensures that the business doesn't just grow in size but also in value, creating a more resilient and prosperous company.

* * *

Step 5: Invest in Personal and Professional Growth

A wealth mindset also involves ongoing personal and professional growth. The more you grow as an individual, the more you can contribute to the growth of your business. Successful entrepreneurs constantly seek to improve their skills, expand their knowledge, and stay updated on industry trends.

Investing in personal growth includes:

Developing leadership skills: Strong leadership is critical for guiding your team and making strategic decisions that impact the business.

Networking: Build relationships with other entrepreneurs, mentors, and industry leaders. These connections can open doors to new opportunities.

Learning about new technologies and trends: Stay ahead of the curve by understanding the latest innovations that can help your business stay competitive.

By continually developing yourself and your skills, you position yourself and your business for sustained success and wealth.

* * *

Step 6: Build a Strong Support Network

No entrepreneur succeeds alone. Building wealth in business requires collaboration, mentorship, and a solid support system. Surround yourself with people who share your vision, challenge your thinking, and offer support when needed. This network can include business partners, mentors, investors, employees, and even family and friends who understand your entrepreneurial journey.

A strong support network can:

Provide guidance during tough decisions

Offer insights that you might not have considered

Help you manage stress and maintain focus

By leveraging the expertise and support of others, you can build a business that is stronger, more resilient, and more likely to achieve long-term prosperity.

* * *

Step 7: Stay Focused on Long-Term Goals

Building wealth through business success is not about chasing quick wins; it's about staying focused on long-term goals. Wealth-building entrepreneurs understand the importance of delayed gratification and are willing to make sacrifices in the short term to reap the rewards later.

Maintain your focus on long-term objectives by:

Setting clear milestones: Break down your long-term goals into smaller, actionable steps that can be tracked over time.

Being patient: Building wealth takes time, and while it's important to seize opportunities, it's equally important to wait for the right moments for growth.

Staying committed: Stick with your vision and goals, even when the path seems challenging or when short-term results are not as expected.

By staying focused on the bigger picture, you ensure that your efforts are aligned with your long-term vision of success and wealth.

* * *

The Wealth Mindset as the Foundation for Entrepreneurial Success

A wealth-focused mindset is the cornerstone of entrepreneurial success. By cultivating a long-term vision, focusing on value creation, practicing sound financial management, and continually growing as an individual, you can build a business that generates lasting wealth.

Entrepreneurs with a wealth mindset embrace challenges, focus on opportunities, and stay committed to their long-term goals. By following these principles, you not only grow your business but also create a legacy of prosperity that can endure for generations. Success is not merely about the money you make—it's about the wealth you build, the impact you create, and the lives you change along the way.

Networking and Its Impact on Wealth

T he Power of Relationships in Wealth Building

In the pursuit of wealth, it's often not just what you know, but who you know that can make all the difference. Networking is more than simply exchanging business cards or making casual acquaintances. It's about building meaningful, mutually beneficial relationships with people who can help you grow, learn, and expand your opportunities. This chapter delves into the importance of networking, how to build a powerful network, and how these connections can play a pivotal role in your wealth-building journey.

* * *

The Wealth Potential of Networking

Networking is often touted as a key factor in entrepreneurial success, but its impact is felt across all aspects of wealth-building. Successful individuals often attribute much of their financial success to the relationships they've cultivated throughout their careers. In the right context, networking can lead to opportunities for investment, partnerships, mentorship, and valuable collaborations—all of which can accelerate your path to prosperity.

It's essential to understand that networking isn't solely about getting something from others; it's about creating a reciprocal exchange of value. Whether it's sharing knowledge, offering support, or making introductions, each interaction within your network has the potential to open doors that would otherwise remain closed.

* * *

Step 1: Understanding the Value of Relationships

The first step in effective networking is recognizing the inherent value of relationships. The people you connect with can offer not just advice, but access to their resources, networks, and knowledge. They can introduce you to influential individuals, inform you of opportunities, or offer insights you may not have considered on your own.

Relationships within your network can serve various purposes:

Mentors provide guidance and wisdom, helping you avoid common mistakes and fast-track your personal and business development.

Peers offer support, motivation, and collaboration. They can challenge you to push your limits and grow alongside you.

Industry experts and influencers open doors to new ideas, trends, and opportunities that could be instrumental in your success.

Each relationship has the potential to contribute to your financial growth, and understanding this value shifts your perspective from transactional interactions to long-term, purpose-driven connections.

* * *

Step 2: Building a Network of Like-Minded Individuals

To leverage networking effectively, it's crucial to surround yourself with people who share your vision or have experiences that align with your goals. This doesn't mean only connecting with people who are exactly like you or are at the same stage of their journey. In fact, diversity in your network—across industries, expertise, and experiences—can provide broader insights and opportunities.

When building your network, prioritize:

People with complementary skills and knowledge: Having individuals in your network who bring different perspectives and areas of expertise can broaden your understanding and open doors to creative collaborations.

People who inspire you: Seek out individuals who challenge you to think bigger, take smarter risks, and believe in your potential.

People who add value: Building relationships with individuals who offer value—whether through knowledge, connections, or advice—will enrich your own understanding and ability to succeed.

As your network grows, focus on creating a group that supports your goals, shares in your vision, and actively contributes to your journey.

* * *

Step 3: The Art of Networking: Connecting with Purpose

Networking is not about collecting as many contacts as possible; it's about building meaningful relationships. The most effective networkers focus on quality over quantity. They approach each connection with a mindset of adding value and fostering trust. The goal is to create a genuine connection where both parties can benefit.

To network effectively:

Be authentic: People are drawn to genuine interactions. Be yourself and approach networking with the intention to build lasting, meaningful relationships.

Offer value before expecting it: Focus on how you can help others before seeking help yourself. Whether it's offering advice, making introductions, or providing resources, showing your willingness to help builds goodwill.

Engage actively: Networking doesn't stop after the first meeting or conversation. Follow up, offer to collaborate, and show interest in the other person's success. Consistency and effort over time are what make relationships thrive.

Networking is a long-term investment. The stronger and more authentic the relationship, the more likely it is to yield positive returns in the future.

* * *

Step 4: Leveraging Your Network for Growth and Wealth

Once you've built a network of strong relationships, it's time to leverage them for your financial growth. Connections within your network can lead to opportunities that directly impact your wealth-building efforts. This can include investment opportunities, collaborations, or valuable business partnerships.

To leverage your network effectively:

Seek strategic partnerships: A strong partnership can help you scale your business, expand into new markets, or access resources that were previously out of reach.

Tap into your network's knowledge: Surrounding yourself with experienced individuals allows you to access insights that can guide your decisions, improve your strategies, and minimize risks.

Identify opportunities: Your network can provide information about potential business ventures, investments, or trends you might not otherwise have known about.

Always remember, leveraging your network is about offering value in return. The more you give, the more you stand to receive.

* * *

Step 5: Expanding Your Network to Create More Opportunities

As you build your network and experience success, it's essential to continue expanding it. The wealthiest individuals are constantly meeting new people and exploring new relationships. This expansion helps them stay ahead of trends, diversify their investment opportunities, and access new resources.

To expand your network:

Attend industry events and conferences: These events provide opportunities to meet influential individuals and stay updated on the latest trends in your industry.

Join professional organizations: Being a part of formal networks or groups gives you a platform to meet like-minded individuals and form meaningful connections.

Utilize social media: Platforms like LinkedIn, Twitter, and even Instagram offer opportunities to connect with thought leaders, potential mentors, and other entrepreneurs.

Expanding your network means exposing yourself to new ideas, perspectives, and opportunities that could significantly accelerate your wealth-building journey.

* * *

Step 6: Networking for Personal Growth

Networking is not just about financial gain—it's also an essential tool for personal growth. By surrounding yourself with successful, driven individuals, you learn and grow in ways you may not have expected. These relationships challenge your thinking, expand your worldview, and inspire you to become a better version of yourself.

Personal growth through networking can:

Help you develop new skills: Whether through mentorship or collaborative work, you will constantly be exposed to new ideas and strategies.

Build resilience: Being part of a supportive network provides a source of motivation, encouragement, and accountability.

Boost confidence: Networking with successful individuals who believe in your potential can increase your self-confidence and inspire you to take bold actions.

By engaging in meaningful connections, you not only gain access to wealth-building opportunities but also enhance your personal development.

* * *

Networking as a Cornerstone of Wealth

Networking is more than just a business strategy; it is a crucial component of wealth-building that connects you to people, resources, and opportunities that can propel you toward financial success. By building and nurturing meaningful relationships, you can leverage your network to create partnerships, gain new insights, and unlock opportunities that would be difficult to access otherwise.

Remember, the key to effective networking is value: offer value to others, and in return, you will gain access to a wealth of resources and opportunities. Networking is not about instant gratification but about building a support system that will pay dividends over time. The more you invest in relationships, the greater the wealth you will accumulate—not just in financial terms, but in knowledge, experience, and opportunities.

The Role of Discipline and Patience

T he Power of Persistence

When we think about building wealth, many are drawn to the idea of quick gains or fast success. However, true wealth is rarely achieved overnight. It requires discipline and patience—two virtues that are often overlooked but are essential for sustaining financial growth and reaching long-term prosperity. In this chapter, we'll explore why discipline and patience are the cornerstones of lasting financial success and how these virtues can keep you on track toward your wealth-building goals.

* * *

The Foundation of Discipline in Wealth Building

Discipline is the ability to control your actions, behavior, and emotions in the face of external demands, to achieve a greater goal. In wealth-building, discipline manifests in several ways, from sticking to a strict savings plan to making intentional investment decisions based on long-term goals. It is about committing to the process, even when the immediate rewards are not apparent.

Wealth-building requires consistent actions, whether it's budgeting, saving a percentage of your income, or investing in your future. It's easy to get distracted by short-term desires or follow fleeting trends, but discipline keeps you focused on your primary objectives.

Key aspects of discipline in wealth-building include:

Sticking to a budget: Understanding your income and expenses and ensuring you live below your means is a daily practice of financial discipline.

Avoiding unnecessary debt: It's tempting to buy things on credit, but disciplined people resist this urge to ensure they don't over-leverage themselves.

Making informed investment decisions: Rather than chasing quick profits, disciplined investors stick to their strategies, even when the market experiences fluctuations.

By practicing discipline, you can ensure that your actions align with your wealth-building goals, leading to a steady path toward prosperity.

* * *

Patience: The Key to Long-Term Success

While discipline is the constant force that keeps you on track, patience is the quality that enables you to stay calm as you wait for your efforts to bear fruit. Building wealth is not an immediate process, and most of the most successful individuals have one thing in common: they understand the value of patience.

In an age of instant gratification, patience can be a difficult virtue to practice. But wealth that is built quickly often dissipates just as fast. True wealth takes time to accumulate. It is about making slow, deliberate decisions and sticking to the plan over the long haul.

Patience in wealth-building means:

Not reacting to market fluctuations: Financial markets go through periods of highs and lows. Instead of panicking, wealthy individuals remain patient and ride out the volatility.

Waiting for investments to mature: Whether it's real estate, stocks, or business ventures, wealth-building investments take time to grow. Patience is what allows you to see the full potential of these assets.

Understanding the compounding effect: The longer you invest and save, the more time your wealth has to grow. Patience allows you to take full advantage of compound interest and other forms of financial growth.

Without patience, it's easy to give up or make impulsive decisions that could harm your financial future. With it, however, you can weather any storm and allow your investments to reach their full potential.

* * *

Discipline and Patience in Daily Life

Building wealth isn't just a matter of large, strategic decisions; it's about how you manage your daily habits. The small, consistent steps you take every day compound over time. Discipline and patience both play vital roles in these daily actions, from how you manage your money to how you approach your financial mindset.

For example, sticking to a budget requires discipline to avoid unnecessary spending, while patience is needed when you feel the temptation to splurge or make impulse purchases. Similarly, investing in a retirement fund or building a real estate portfolio requires the same two virtues: discipline in making regular contributions and patience in waiting for the long-term growth.

* * *

Staying Committed to Your Financial Goals

It's easy to set financial goals, but the true challenge lies in remaining committed to them, especially when life presents challenges or distractions. This is where discipline shines—by making daily, conscious decisions that align with your objectives.

But even with discipline, there will be times when the road to wealth seems long, and progress appears slow. During these moments, patience is essential. Remember that success doesn't happen overnight, and wealth isn't built in a day. By staying patient, you acknowledge that your efforts will pay off, even when results aren't immediate.

There will be moments when the financial path is not as smooth, and unexpected expenses or setbacks may arise. It is in these moments that both discipline and patience come into play. Staying disciplined will keep you on track, even when the temptation to abandon your plan is strong. Patience will allow you to stay calm, knowing that temporary setbacks are just a part of the process.

* * *

The Role of Patience in Investment Strategies

One of the most critical areas where patience is necessary is in investing. Many investors make the mistake of trying to time the market, jumping in and out based on short-term trends or fears. This is often a result of impatience, and it can hinder wealth-building over time.

Patience in investing means resisting the urge to sell at the first sign of a market downturn or to buy into the latest "hot" trend without proper research. Instead, successful investors stay the course with a well-thought-out strategy that aligns with their long-term goals.

Here are key examples where patience plays a role:

Stock market investing: Long-term investors often see the most success. Holding onto investments for years rather than making quick moves based on market noise ensures more consistent and stable returns.

Real estate investing: Real estate typically appreciates over time. Being patient enough to hold onto properties through market cycles allows you to take advantage of long-term growth.

Business growth: Building a successful business takes time. Growing your business slowly and consistently allows you to maintain control and avoid taking unnecessary risks.

By making strategic, long-term investments and allowing time for these investments to grow, you will be on the path to wealth accumulation.

* * *

Developing Financial Discipline and Patience

Both financial discipline and patience are learned behaviors. They require intentional practice and self-control. The good news is that both can be developed with time, awareness, and commitment. The following steps can help you strengthen these two key virtues:

Set clear, actionable goals: Knowing exactly what you're working toward makes it easier to stay disciplined and patient. Break larger goals into smaller, achievable steps.

Create systems and routines: Systems help ensure that you consistently make the right decisions. Whether it's a weekly budget review, automated savings, or a regular investment schedule, building systems can help you stay disciplined.

Practice mindfulness and delayed gratification: Patience is often a matter of managing your emotions and impulses. Practicing mindfulness or simply pausing to reflect before making a financial decision can help you avoid knee-jerk reactions.

Track your progress: Regularly reviewing your financial progress helps you see how far you've come. This can boost your patience when things seem slow.

As you practice discipline and patience, you'll begin to notice a shift in your mindset and approach. Both virtues will become second nature, and they will work together to keep you on the path to lasting wealth.

* * *

Wealth Is a Journey, Not a Sprint

The road to lifelong wealth is not a race—it's a journey. While ambition and enthusiasm are important, they must be tempered by the steady hand of discipline and the calm of patience. By committing to consistent action and remaining patient as you progress, you'll be able to weather challenges and capitalize on opportunities as they arise.

Incorporating both discipline and patience into your daily financial habits will set you apart from those who seek shortcuts. These virtues will keep you grounded and focused on what truly matters: long-term wealth accumulation and financial independence.

Remember, achieving wealth is not about instant gratification. It's about making the right decisions day by day, year by year, and trusting that your hard work will eventually pay off. The combination of discipline and patience ensures that you'll stay the course, no matter the obstacles that come your way.

Setting Realistic Financial Goals

The Power of Clear Goals

T he path to prosperity begins with a clear vision of where you want to go. Without goals, financial success becomes a distant dream rather than a structured, achievable reality. Setting realistic financial goals provides you with direction and purpose, ensuring that your actions align with your long-term vision. In this chapter, we will explore how to set effective, realistic financial goals using the SMART framework, a proven method that will guide your journey toward financial success.

* * *

The Importance of Goal Setting in Wealth Building

Goals are not just abstract ideas; they are the blueprint for your financial journey. Whether it's saving for retirement, buying a home, or building an investment portfolio, each financial goal plays a crucial role in shaping your financial future. Without clear goals, it's easy to lose focus and be distracted by immediate desires or external pressures.

A goal without a plan is merely a wish. To truly build wealth, you need more than just a vague desire for financial freedom. You need a clear, actionable plan with well-defined goals that can be measured and achieved over time.

Setting financial goals enables you to:

Track progress: Clear goals allow you to measure how far you've come and what needs to be done next.

Prioritize resources: Knowing what you're working toward helps you allocate your money and time effectively.

Stay motivated: A well-defined goal provides something tangible to work toward, helping you stay focused and energized.

* * *

Understanding the SMART Goal Framework

The SMART goal-setting framework is one of the most effective tools for ensuring your goals are both achievable and actionable. SMART stands for Specific, Measurable, Achievable, Relevant, and Time-bound. This structure helps transform vague objectives into clear, actionable targets that can be achieved systematically.

Here's a breakdown of each component:

Specific: Your goal should be clear and focused. Avoid vague objectives like "save more money." Instead, specify the amount you want to save and the purpose behind it. For example, "Save $10,000 for a down payment on a home."

Measurable: A measurable goal allows you to track progress. Instead of saying, "Invest more," a measurable goal would be "Invest $500 every month in my retirement account."

Achievable: Set goals that are realistic, given your current financial situation. While it's good to challenge yourself, setting an unachievable goal can lead to frustration. For example, if you're just starting, a goal of saving $1 million in a year may not be realistic, but saving $5,000 in six months might be.

Relevant: Ensure that your financial goals align with your overall values and long-term objectives. A goal should contribute to your broader vision of wealth and prosperity.

Time-bound: Set deadlines for your goals. Without a clear timeline, goals can remain abstract and unachievable. For example, "Save $10,000 for a down payment within the next 12 months."

By using the SMART framework, your goals become more than just a wish—they become a plan with clear steps to follow.

* * *

How to Break Down Long-Term Goals into Manageable Steps

Long-term financial goals, such as saving for retirement or building wealth through investments, can often feel overwhelming. However, breaking these goals down into smaller, more manageable steps can make them feel more achievable. It's important to remember that achieving wealth is a marathon, not a sprint. Each small, incremental step adds up over time.

For example, if your goal is to save $100,000 for retirement in 15 years, break this down into yearly, monthly, and even weekly savings targets. Instead of focusing on the big number, you'll feel more empowered as you consistently hit your smaller milestones.

To break down long-term goals effectively:

Set annual goals: If your goal is $100,000 in 15 years, aim for $6,666 per year.

Establish monthly targets: Divide the annual goal by 12 months, setting a monthly savings or investment target.

Track progress regularly: Review your goals quarterly or bi-annually to ensure you're on track and make adjustments as needed.

* * *

Aligning Goals with Your Current Financial Situation

Setting realistic goals also requires an honest assessment of where you currently stand financially. Understanding your income, expenses, debts, and current savings allows you to determine what goals are achievable and how much effort will be required to achieve them.

Begin by tracking your monthly cash flow:

Income: What's your monthly income after taxes?

Expenses: What are your fixed and variable monthly expenses?

Debt: Do you have any high-interest debt that needs to be paid off before you can start saving or investing?

Once you have a clear understanding of your financial situation, you can allocate funds to different goals. For instance, paying off high-interest debt should be prioritized over investing if you're in significant debt, as the interest on the debt will outpace any investment returns in the short term.

* * *

Prioritizing Your Financial Goals

Not all goals are created equal. Some may be more urgent or important than others. For instance, paying off high-interest credit card debt is likely a higher priority than saving for a vacation. The key is to balance short-term goals, like eliminating debt, with long-term goals, like investing for retirement.

Here are some tips for prioritizing your financial goals:

Use the 80/20 Rule: Focus 80% of your energy on your most important financial goals. This might mean prioritizing building an emergency fund or contributing to retirement savings.

Factor in time: Short-term goals (like buying a car) can often be achieved more quickly than long-term goals (like buying a home). Adjust your focus based on the timeline.

Stay flexible: Life changes, and so might your financial situation. Be ready to adjust your goals as needed, without abandoning them entirely.

* * *

Common Mistakes to Avoid When Setting Financial Goals

While goal-setting is crucial for wealth building, it's also easy to make mistakes that can hinder progress. Some common mistakes to avoid include:

Setting unrealistic goals: Aim for goals that are ambitious but attainable. If your goals are too large or vague, you might become discouraged.

Neglecting to track progress: If you don't track your progress regularly, it's easy to lose sight of your goals or underestimate the time and effort required.

Lack of flexibility: Your goals should evolve as your financial situation changes. Life events like a job change, marriage, or having children can impact your goals and how you achieve them.

Failure to plan for obstacles: The road to prosperity is rarely smooth. Planning for potential setbacks—such as emergencies or unexpected expenses—will ensure that you remain focused on your goals even when life gets in the way.

* * *

Celebrating Milestones and Achievements

While it's important to remain focused on long-term goals, don't forget to celebrate small victories along the way. Achieving milestones, whether it's paying off a debt, saving a certain amount, or hitting an investment target, is a testament to your commitment. Celebrating these achievements not only boosts your morale but reinforces positive financial behaviors.

Remember, the journey to financial success is not just about the destination; it's also about acknowledging and enjoying the process.

* * *

Stay Focused and Committed

Setting realistic financial goals is the first step toward building a prosperous future. By using the SMART framework, breaking down long-term goals into manageable steps, and aligning your goals with your current financial situation, you can ensure that you're always moving forward.

While achieving wealth requires time, discipline, and patience, a clear, actionable plan makes the journey more manageable and rewarding. Stay focused on your goals, track your progress, and adjust as needed. Over time, your consistent efforts will lead to the lasting prosperity you seek.

Protecting Your Wealth Through Insurance

W hy Insurance Matters in Wealth Protection

Building wealth is a monumental achievement, but wealth without protection is vulnerable to unexpected risks. One of the most effective ways to safeguard your financial future is through insurance. Insurance is a tool that can help you manage life's uncertainties, ensuring that your wealth is not depleted by events beyond your control. In this chapter, we will explore the different types of insurance that serve as essential safeguards, protecting your wealth from financial loss caused by unforeseen events.

* * *

Understanding the Role of Insurance in Wealth Protection

Insurance plays a critical role in wealth protection by providing a safety net. Whether it's medical bills after an accident, damages to property, or the loss of income due to illness or death, insurance helps mitigate the financial consequences of life's most unexpected challenges. It can ensure that a single event doesn't derail your long-term financial goals and that your wealth remains intact for future generations.

The essence of insurance is simple: pay a manageable premium regularly in exchange for financial coverage should you face an adverse situation. This approach allows you to prevent large, unexpected expenses from causing irreversible damage to your wealth.

* * *

Types of Insurance to Protect Your Wealth

There are several types of insurance designed to protect different aspects of your wealth. While not every type of insurance is necessary for everyone, understanding your unique financial situation and risks is crucial in selecting the right coverage. Here are the most common types of insurance that are vital for wealth protection:

1. Health Insurance

Health insurance is an essential safeguard against rising medical costs. Medical emergencies can quickly deplete your savings, but with the right health insurance, your medical expenses can be covered, leaving your wealth intact. In some countries, having health insurance is mandatory, but even if it's not, securing comprehensive health coverage can protect your finances in case of unexpected illnesses or accidents.

2. Life Insurance

Life insurance provides a financial safety net for your dependents in the event of your death. It ensures that your loved ones will have the financial resources they need to maintain their standard of living without the burden of your financial obligations. Term life insurance provides coverage for a specific period, while whole life insurance covers you for life and often includes a cash value component that grows over time. Life insurance is a critical tool for individuals with dependents or significant debts.

3. Disability Insurance

Disability insurance offers protection if you are unable to work due to illness or injury. Without an income, it can be difficult to maintain your financial commitments. Disability insurance helps replace lost income, allowing you to cover living expenses, debt repayments, and other financial obligations while you focus on recovery. This insurance is particularly important for entrepreneurs or individuals who rely heavily on their ability to work for income.

4. Homeowners or Renters Insurance

Homeowners insurance protects your property against damage or loss from events such as fires, theft, or natural disasters. It also covers liability in case someone is injured on your property. Renters insurance, though often overlooked, is equally important for individuals renting a home. It covers personal property in case of theft, fire, or other damages, and provides liability protection.

5. Auto Insurance

Auto insurance is required in most places and is designed to protect your financial interests in case of car accidents or theft. Liability coverage helps pay for damages you cause to others, while collision and comprehensive coverage protect your own vehicle. Having sufficient auto insurance ensures that the costs associated with accidents or damages do not come out of your pocket, preventing potential setbacks to your wealth.

6. Long-Term Care Insurance

Long-term care insurance is important as you age, helping to cover the costs associated with assisted living or nursing home care. While health insurance and Medicare may cover certain medical expenses, they do not usually cover long-term care. This insurance is particularly important for those looking to protect their wealth in their later years, as long-term care can be expensive and deplete your assets quickly.

7. Umbrella Insurance

Umbrella insurance is a type of liability insurance that provides additional coverage beyond the limits of your other policies, such as auto or homeowners insurance. This type of insurance can protect you from major lawsuits or claims that exceed the standard coverage of your other policies, providing an extra layer of protection against catastrophic financial losses.

8. Business Insurance

For business owners, having adequate business insurance is essential to protect against risks such as property damage, liability claims, and loss of income due to business interruptions. Business insurance can take many forms, including general liability insurance, property insurance, and workers' compensation insurance. This coverage ensures that your business can continue to operate and protect your personal wealth in the event of unforeseen circumstances.

* * *

How to Choose the Right Insurance for Your Situation

Selecting the right insurance depends on your specific financial situation, risk tolerance, and the value of the assets you wish to protect. Here are some guidelines for determining which insurance policies are essential for you:

Assess Your Risks: Consider your life stage and the risks associated with your current lifestyle. For example, if you have young children or a mortgage, life insurance may be a priority. If you're a business owner, you may need business insurance to protect against disruptions.

Evaluate Your Assets: Protect assets such as your home, car, savings, and investments by ensuring you have adequate coverage. For instance, if you own a home, homeowners insurance is crucial to protect the property's value and your investment.

Review Your Financial Situation: Consider how much premium you can comfortably afford without straining your finances. The goal is to

146

balance adequate protection with affordability.

Consult a Financial Advisor: A financial advisor can help you determine which types of insurance are necessary based on your goals and risk profile. They can also provide recommendations for policy amounts, helping you avoid overpaying or under-insuring yourself.

* * *

The Cost of Not Having Insurance

While insurance premiums may seem like an added expense, the cost of not having adequate coverage can be far greater. Without insurance, you risk losing substantial amounts of wealth due to unforeseen events. Medical bills, car accidents, or home repairs can quickly deplete savings, derail retirement plans, or even lead to bankruptcy.

Consider this: If you don't have health insurance and face a major medical emergency, you could be left with hundreds of thousands of dollars in medical debt. Without life insurance, your loved ones may be forced to sell assets or take on debt to maintain their lifestyle after your passing. These are just a few examples of how a lack of insurance can erode your wealth over time.

* * *

Building a Balanced Portfolio of Insurance Coverage

The key to protecting your wealth is to strike a balance between adequate coverage and affordability. Insurance should be seen as an essential tool in wealth management rather than an unnecessary expense. By diversifying your insurance coverage across the different areas of your life—health, home, car, business, and personal liability—you ensure that your wealth remains secure from multiple angles.

As you grow your wealth and accumulate more assets, it's important to periodically review and update your insurance policies. Changes in your life circumstances, such as marriage, children, purchasing property, or starting a business, will necessitate adjustments to your coverage. Regularly assess your policies to ensure they continue to align with your evolving financial goals.

***

Insurance as Part of a Holistic Wealth Strategy

Insurance is not just an afterthought but an essential component of a holistic wealth-building strategy. By protecting yourself, your family, and your assets with the right insurance, you create a safety net that ensures your wealth remains secure, no matter what challenges life throws your way. Whether it's health insurance to cover medical emergencies, life insurance to provide for your loved ones, or business insurance to protect your enterprise, each type of coverage plays a crucial role in maintaining financial stability.

When integrated into a well-rounded financial plan, insurance safeguards your journey toward lifelong prosperity, allowing you to focus on building wealth without fear of unexpected setbacks.

The Importance of Estate Planning

Securing Your Legacy

Wealth accumulation is only one part of the equation when it comes to creating lifelong prosperity. Equally important is ensuring that your hard-earned wealth is preserved, protected, and passed down to future generations. Estate planning is the key to achieving this goal. It allows you to have control over how your assets are distributed after your death, ensuring that your legacy is protected, your loved ones are taken care of, and your wishes are honored.

Estate planning is not just for the wealthy. Regardless of the size of your estate, planning for the future is a responsible and essential step toward safeguarding your wealth and the financial well-being of those you care about. In this chapter, we will explore the basics of estate planning, including wills, trusts, and succession planning, and how they can help you secure your legacy.

* * *

What Is Estate Planning?

Estate planning is the process of organizing your affairs so that, after your death, your assets are distributed according to your wishes. It also involves making decisions about how your financial and medical matters should be handled in case of incapacitation. The core of estate planning revolves around your desire to ensure that your wealth is transferred seamlessly and without unnecessary legal hurdles or tax burdens.

Estate planning provides peace of mind for you and your loved ones, knowing that your financial matters are in order. It's about more than just distributing assets—it's about creating a lasting impact, providing for your family, and ensuring that your wealth continues to work for future generations.

* * *

The Essential Components of Estate Planning

There are several key documents and strategies that make up a comprehensive estate plan. Let's break down each component and its role in protecting your wealth and ensuring your legacy.

1. Wills

A will is a legal document that outlines your wishes regarding the distribution of your assets after your death. It allows you to name beneficiaries who will receive your property, as well as designate guardians for minor children, if applicable. Without a will, your estate may be subject to intestate succession laws, meaning your property will be distributed according to state law rather than your wishes. This can lead to delays and disputes, which can diminish the value of your estate.

When creating a will, it's important to list all assets clearly, including property, financial accounts, and personal belongings. You should also designate an executor to oversee the distribution of your estate and ensure that your wishes are carried out as planned. Revisiting your will periodically is necessary, particularly after major life events such as marriage, divorce, or the birth of a child.

2. Trusts

A trust is a legal arrangement in which one party (the trustee) holds assets on behalf of another (the beneficiary). Trusts are often used as an estate planning tool because they offer advantages that a simple will cannot. One of the main benefits of a trust is that it can help avoid probate, the legal process by which a court determines the validity of a will and distributes assets accordingly. Probate can be time-consuming, costly, and public, but assets held in a trust generally bypass this process, ensuring a quicker and more private transfer of wealth.

There are two main types of trusts:

Revocable Living Trust: This type of trust allows you to retain control of your assets while you're alive and make changes as needed. Upon your death, the assets in the trust pass directly to the beneficiaries, avoiding probate. This is an effective tool for individuals who want to retain flexibility but ensure a smooth transfer of assets.

Irrevocable Trust: This type of trust cannot be modified or revoked once established. While it offers more asset protection and potential tax benefits, it also means you relinquish control over the assets placed in the trust. Irrevocable trusts are commonly used for wealth preservation, especially in cases of estate tax planning or asset protection.

3. Succession Planning

Succession planning is a critical component for those with business interests. It's the process of determining how ownership and management of your business will be transferred after your death or in the event you become incapacitated. Without a solid succession plan, the future of your business can be uncertain, potentially leading to disputes or a loss of control over operations.

A comprehensive succession plan includes identifying successors, creating a framework for the transition of leadership, and addressing how assets related to the business will be divided. In some cases, a trust can be used to facilitate the transfer of business interests and provide for the long-term continuity of the company. An advisor with experience in business succession can help you navigate this process.

4. Power of Attorney (POA)

A Power of Attorney (POA) allows you to appoint someone to

make financial or medical decisions on your behalf if you become incapacitated. There are two main types of POA: a financial POA and a healthcare POA. These documents are essential for ensuring that your wishes are respected during times when you may not be able to advocate for yourself.

A POA is particularly important for those with significant assets, as it ensures that your financial matters are handled appropriately should you be unable to manage them. Similarly, a healthcare POA allows you to designate someone to make medical decisions based on your preferences, ensuring that your health care choices are in alignment with your values.

5. Living Will

A living will is a document that outlines your preferences for medical treatment in the event that you become terminally ill or incapacitated. Unlike a healthcare POA, which designates someone to make decisions on your behalf, a living will provides specific instructions regarding life support, resuscitation, and other medical interventions. Having a living will in place ensures that your healthcare decisions are clear and respected, relieving your loved ones from having to make difficult decisions during a stressful time.

* * *

The Tax Implications of Estate Planning

One of the primary goals of estate planning is to minimize the tax burden on your estate. The estate tax is a tax on the transfer of wealth from one generation to the next, and depending on the value of your estate, this tax can significantly erode the amount passed down to your heirs. The good news is that there are several strategies for reducing estate taxes, including:

Lifetime Gifting: Giving gifts during your lifetime can help reduce the value of your estate and lower the estate tax liability. There are limits to how much you can gift tax-free each year, but these contributions can add up over time.

Establishing Trusts: Trusts, particularly irrevocable trusts, can help remove assets from your taxable estate, reducing the estate tax burden. By placing assets in a trust, you effectively reduce the estate's value at the time of your death, which can lead to lower taxes.

Charitable Donations: Donating to charity during your lifetime or through your estate plan can provide tax deductions and reduce the overall value of your taxable estate.

A tax advisor or estate planner can help you develop a strategy that minimizes taxes and maximizes the wealth passed on to your heirs.

* * *

The Importance of Regularly Reviewing Your Estate Plan

Estate planning is not a one-time event. Your financial situation, family circumstances, and goals may change over time, so it's essential to regularly review and update your estate plan. Major life events such as marriage, divorce, the birth of children, or changes in assets should prompt a review of your plan to ensure it remains aligned with your wishes.

If you move to a different state or country, it's especially important to revisit your estate plan, as laws regarding inheritance, taxes, and probate may differ. An estate plan that is updated regularly ensures that your legacy is preserved according to your current desires, not outdated instructions.

* * *

Ensuring a Lasting Legacy

Estate planning is a critical element of wealth preservation and legacy-building. By taking the time to create a comprehensive plan, you ensure that your wealth is passed down smoothly to future generations, without the delays, complications, or taxes that can erode its value. Whether through a will, trust, or business succession plan, the right estate plan provides clarity, protects your assets, and gives your loved ones peace of mind.

By investing the time and effort into estate planning now, you lay the foundation for a lasting legacy that continues to benefit your family and community long after you're gone. Protecting your wealth is not only a financial necessity—it's a moral responsibility to those you care about, ensuring that the fruits of your labor benefit future generations and contribute to their own prosperity.

Understanding Tax Strategies for Wealth Preservation

The Impact of Taxes on Wealth

Taxes are a significant factor that can affect the growth and preservation of your wealth. While paying taxes is a necessary part of society, understanding the strategies available to minimize your tax liability can help protect your assets, increase your savings, and ensure that your wealth is preserved over time. The key is to approach tax planning strategically, with a focus on reducing taxable income, taking advantage of tax incentives, and utilizing legal strategies to protect and grow your wealth.

In this chapter, we will explore various tax strategies designed to help you minimize taxes legally while preserving your wealth for the long term. These strategies are designed to work within the existing tax laws and can be applied across a variety of financial situations, from personal savings to business investments.

* * *

1. Understanding Your Taxable Income

The first step in any tax strategy is understanding what constitutes taxable income. In simple terms, taxable income is the income you earn that is subject to taxation. This includes wages, interest, dividends, capital gains, and other sources of income. The higher your taxable income, the higher the tax liability.

To begin minimizing taxes, it is important to assess your sources of income and identify ways to reduce them. For example:

Tax-Deferred Accounts: Contributing to tax-deferred accounts such as a 401(k) or IRA reduces your taxable income in the year you contribute. This means that your contribution amount is deducted from your taxable income, lowering the overall tax burden for that year.

Tax-Free Accounts: Tax-free accounts, like Roth IRAs or Roth 401(k)s, allow you to contribute after-tax income but benefit from tax-free withdrawals in retirement. These accounts are an excellent long-term strategy for wealth preservation as they help reduce taxable income in the future.

By understanding what types of income are taxed and how to leverage tax-advantaged accounts, you can create a strategy that minimizes taxes while maximizing savings.

* * *

2. Tax-Advantaged Accounts for Wealth Building

One of the most effective ways to reduce taxes and preserve wealth is by utilizing tax-advantaged accounts. These accounts are specifically designed to help individuals save for retirement or other long-term goals while benefiting from tax incentives.

Individual Retirement Accounts (IRAs): Traditional IRAs allow you to make tax-deductible contributions, which reduce your taxable income for the year. The investments grow tax-deferred until withdrawal, at which point they are taxed as ordinary income. Roth IRAs, on the other hand, do not provide a tax deduction for contributions but allow your investments to grow and be withdrawn tax-free in retirement.

401(k) Plans: A 401(k) plan allows you to contribute pre-tax income to your retirement fund, reducing your current taxable income. In addition to the tax benefits, many employers offer matching contributions, which is essentially free money to help you build wealth.

Health Savings Accounts (HSAs): HSAs are a tax-advantaged way to save for medical expenses. Contributions are made on a pre-tax basis, meaning they lower your taxable income, and withdrawals for qualified medical expenses are tax-free. Additionally, any unused funds in an HSA can be carried over year after year, making it an excellent long-term strategy.

529 College Savings Plans: If you have children and are saving for their education, a 529 plan offers tax-free growth and tax-free withdrawals

when used for qualified education expenses. This strategy helps reduce the tax burden while contributing to long-term wealth goals.

By regularly contributing to these tax-advantaged accounts, you can reduce your taxable income, grow your wealth, and protect your assets for the future.

* * *

3. Capital Gains Tax Minimization

Capital gains taxes are taxes applied to the profit from the sale of assets like stocks, bonds, or real estate. The tax rate on capital gains depends on how long the asset was held before being sold:

Short-Term Capital Gains: If you sell an asset that you've held for less than a year, you'll be taxed at the same rate as your ordinary income tax rate, which can be quite high.

Long-Term Capital Gains: If you hold an asset for more than a year before selling, the profits are taxed at a reduced rate, typically ranging from 0% to 20%, depending on your income level.

To minimize the tax impact of capital gains, consider the following strategies:

Hold Investments Long-Term: Whenever possible, hold your investments for more than a year before selling to benefit from the lower long-term capital gains tax rate.

Tax-Loss Harvesting: Tax-loss harvesting involves selling investments that have decreased in value to offset gains realized from other investments. This strategy can reduce your taxable income by offsetting capital gains with losses.

Like-Kind Exchange: For real estate investors, a like-kind exchange allows you to defer taxes on capital gains when selling property, as long as the proceeds are reinvested into a similar property. This strategy is particularly useful for real estate investors looking to grow their portfolio without immediately incurring a tax burden.

* * *

4. Taking Advantage of Deductions and Credits

Deductions and tax credits are powerful tools for reducing your overall tax burden. Deductions reduce your taxable income, while tax credits directly reduce the amount of taxes you owe. Here are some key deductions and credits to consider:

Standard Deduction vs. Itemized Deductions: The IRS offers a standard deduction, which automatically reduces your taxable income by a set amount. However, if your qualifying expenses (such as mortgage interest, medical expenses, or charitable contributions) exceed the standard deduction, you may benefit from itemizing deductions.

Business Deductions: For business owners, there are numerous deductions available to reduce taxable income. This includes deductions for business expenses such as office supplies, marketing costs, and travel expenses. Taking full advantage of these deductions can help reduce your overall tax liability.

Charitable Contributions: Donating to charity can provide tax deductions that reduce your taxable income. Charitable donations are a great way to lower taxes while supporting causes you care about.

Tax Credits: Tax credits directly reduce the amount of taxes you owe. Examples include the Child Tax Credit, Education Tax Credits, and the Earned Income Tax Credit. These credits can provide significant savings for eligible taxpayers.

* * *

5. Estate and Gift Tax Planning

When it comes to preserving wealth, one of the most important tax considerations is the estate and gift tax. The estate tax is levied on the value of your estate when you pass away, while the gift tax is applied to the transfer of assets during your lifetime.

To minimize the tax impact of both, consider the following strategies:

Lifetime Gifting: One way to reduce your taxable estate is by gifting assets to family members during your lifetime. The IRS allows you to gift a certain amount each year without triggering gift taxes. These annual gifts can reduce the value of your estate and minimize future estate taxes.

Establishing Trusts: Irrevocable trusts can be used to remove assets from your taxable estate, ensuring they are passed on to beneficiaries without incurring estate taxes. Trusts also provide greater control over how your assets are distributed.

Taking Advantage of the Estate Tax Exemption: The IRS allows a significant estate tax exemption, which allows you to pass a certain amount of wealth to heirs without incurring estate taxes. By planning ahead, you can ensure that your estate falls below the exemption limit, thereby reducing or eliminating estate taxes.

* * *

6. Consulting with a Tax Professional

Navigating the complexities of tax strategies can be overwhelming, which is why it's important to work with a tax professional. A certified public accountant (CPA) or tax advisor can help you identify the best strategies to minimize taxes based on your unique financial situation.

They can also help you stay updated on changes to tax laws and ensure that you are in full compliance with all applicable regulations.

* * *

Preserving Wealth Through Strategic Tax Planning

Taxes are an inevitable part of wealth creation and preservation, but they don't have to be a roadblock to your financial success. By employing strategic tax planning, utilizing tax-advantaged accounts, minimizing capital gains taxes, and taking advantage of deductions and credits, you can significantly reduce your tax burden and protect your wealth for the long term. Remember, the key is to be proactive, stay informed, and consult with professionals who can guide you toward the best tax strategies for your unique financial goals. By doing so, you can ensure that your wealth continues to grow and be passed down to future generations without being unduly diminished by taxes.

The Art of Negotiation in Wealth Building

The Power of Negotiation in Wealth Building

Negotiation is not just a business skill—it is an essential tool for wealth building. Whether you are negotiating business contracts, investments, or even personal finance decisions, the ability to negotiate effectively can significantly impact your financial outcomes. A successful negotiation can help you secure better deals, save money, and create opportunities that may otherwise be missed. In this chapter, we will explore the techniques that can help you become a more confident and effective negotiator, enabling you to unlock new wealth-building possibilities.

* * *

1. The Importance of Preparation

One of the key elements of successful negotiation is preparation.

Before entering any negotiation, it is crucial to gather as much information as possible. This includes understanding the parties involved, the context of the deal, and the potential outcomes. Being prepared allows you to identify areas where you have leverage, anticipate objections, and decide in advance what your ideal outcome is.

Know Your Worth: Whether you're negotiating a salary, a business deal, or an investment, understanding your value is critical. This knowledge gives you confidence and ensures you don't settle for less than you deserve.

Research the Other Party: Understanding the other party's needs and constraints can give you a strategic advantage. By knowing their motivations, you can craft your proposals in a way that appeals to their interests while still achieving your goals.

Set Your Goals and Limits: Define your objectives clearly. Know what you want to achieve, and also understand your walk-away point—this is the point where you are no longer willing to continue with the deal.

* * *

2. Building Rapport and Trust

Building rapport is a fundamental aspect of successful negotiation. When both parties feel comfortable and trust each other, the negotiation process becomes more collaborative rather than adversarial. Trust can often lead to better deals for both sides, as it paves the way for open communication and a mutual desire to reach an agreement.

Active Listening: Listening attentively to the other party is crucial. By understanding their needs, you can find ways to address them while also advancing your own interests. Listening shows respect and helps you identify common ground.

Empathy and Understanding: Demonstrating empathy can help create a positive environment for negotiation. When the other party feels understood, they may be more inclined to be flexible and open to your proposals.

* * *

3. Leverage and Power Dynamics

In every negotiation, there are power dynamics at play. The goal is not to overpower the other party, but rather to recognize where you have leverage and use it effectively. Leverage can take many forms, such as financial resources, knowledge, timing, or even alternatives to the deal being negotiated.

Identify Your Leverage: What gives you an advantage? It could be the ability to offer a better deal, an alternative solution, or a unique resource. Recognizing your leverage allows you to negotiate from a position of strength.

Use Anchoring Effectively: Anchoring refers to the tactic of starting the negotiation with a high or low initial offer to set the tone for the entire negotiation. The first offer often influences the rest of the discussions, so use this tactic wisely.

Timing: The timing of your offer can also be a source of leverage. Negotiating at the right time—such as when the other party is under pressure or eager to close a deal—can give you an advantage.

* * *

4. Finding Win-Win Solutions

Great negotiators aim for win-win outcomes where both parties feel they have gained something valuable. A win-win scenario fosters long-term relationships and ensures that both sides are satisfied with the outcome. This approach often leads to more sustainable and productive partnerships, which are essential for wealth-building.

Focus on Interests, Not Positions: In many negotiations, each side starts with a position—what they want. However, focusing on underlying interests (the reasons behind those positions) can create more flexibility and open up creative solutions that satisfy both parties.

Look for Trade-Offs: In negotiations, it is important to consider what you are willing to give up in exchange for what you want. Often, compromises are necessary, but by focusing on trade-offs, you can achieve a mutually beneficial outcome.

Be Creative in Problem-Solving: If the deal seems stuck, think outside the box. Look for alternative ways to meet both parties' needs, such as adjusting timelines, payment structures, or additional perks.

* * *

5. Handling Objections and Difficult Situations

In any negotiation, objections and difficult situations will arise. How you handle these challenges can determine the success of the deal. Being calm, composed, and ready with responses is essential.

Stay Calm and Patient: Don't react impulsively to objections or pushback. Take time to assess the situation and respond thoughtfully. Sometimes, silence can be an effective tool—pausing after an objection gives you time to think and often leads the other party to offer additional information or concessions.

Counter-Offer Tactfully: When you receive a counteroffer that doesn't meet your expectations, respond by explaining why your original proposal was beneficial. Provide logical reasons, backed by facts, to support your stance.

Know When to Walk Away: Sometimes, despite your best efforts, the negotiation may not be heading in the right direction. If you've reached your limit or the deal no longer serves your interests, be prepared to walk away. Walking away doesn't mean giving up; it means recognizing when the deal isn't worth pursuing.

* * *

6. Closing the Deal

The final step in a successful negotiation is closing the deal. A great negotiator knows when to bring the conversation to a close and how to ensure that both parties feel satisfied with the outcome.

Seal the Deal with Confidence: Once you've reached an agreement, don't hesitate to finalize the terms. Reaffirm the key points and ensure that both parties are clear on the next steps. Be confident in your decision, as this signals professionalism and decisiveness.

Document the Agreement: Whether verbal or written, it's important to have a record of the agreement. In business and investments, a formal contract or written agreement ensures that both parties are legally bound to the terms.

Follow Through: After the deal is closed, it's important to honor your commitments. Following through on your promises builds credibility and trust, which are essential for maintaining long-term wealth-building relationships.

* * *

Mastering Negotiation for Long-Term Wealth

Negotiation is more than just a skill—it is an art that plays a crucial role in wealth building. By preparing thoroughly, building rapport, recognizing leverage, seeking win-win solutions, handling objections gracefully, and closing deals confidently, you can unlock new financial opportunities and secure better outcomes in business, investments, and personal finance. Mastering negotiation empowers you to not only grow your wealth but also create lasting relationships that will support your financial goals in the long run. Whether you're negotiating a business contract or a personal deal, negotiation is an invaluable tool that can drive your path to prosperity.

Taking Advantage of Technology in Wealth Creation

E mbracing Technology for Financial Growth

In today's fast-paced world, technology has revolutionized the way we manage money, invest, and create wealth. From financial apps and investment platforms to automation tools and online resources, the digital age provides countless opportunities to streamline financial management and grow your wealth. Understanding how to leverage these tools effectively can accelerate your journey to financial success. In this chapter, we will explore how technology can empower you in various areas of wealth creation, from tracking expenses to making intelligent investment decisions.

* * *

1. Financial Apps for Budgeting and Tracking Expenses

One of the first steps in wealth creation is mastering the art of budgeting. Financial apps have simplified this process, making it easier to track expenses, set financial goals, and stick to a budget. These apps can help you understand where your money is going, highlight areas for improvement, and provide insights into how to save more effectively.

Personal Finance Apps: Tools like Mint, YNAB (You Need a Budget), and PocketGuard allow you to connect your bank accounts, credit cards, and bills to track spending in real-time. These apps categorize your expenses automatically and provide detailed reports, making it easier to spot spending patterns and identify areas to cut back.

Expense Categorization: By categorizing your expenses, you can better understand your cash flow and pinpoint opportunities for saving. Many financial apps also allow you to set spending limits, helping you adhere to your budget and avoid overspending.

Financial Goal Setting: Setting financial goals is crucial for wealth building. Apps like Qapital and Simple allow you to create specific savings targets (e.g., saving for a vacation, building an emergency fund) and automatically transfer money to dedicated savings accounts based on your goals.

* * *

2. Investment Platforms and Robo-Advisors

Investing is one of the most effective ways to build long-term wealth, and technology has made investing more accessible than ever before. With the rise of investment platforms and robo-advisors, individuals can now start investing with minimal experience and at lower costs than traditional investment methods.

Online Brokerage Accounts: Platforms like E*TRADE, Robinhood, and Fidelity provide users with access to a wide range of investment options, including stocks, ETFs, and bonds. These platforms often feature user-friendly interfaces, educational resources, and low fees, making them an excellent choice for new investors.

Robo-Advisors: Robo-advisors like Betterment and Wealthfront use algorithms to create and manage diversified investment portfolios tailored to your risk tolerance and financial goals. These platforms are a cost-effective way to invest without needing the expertise of a traditional financial advisor. They automatically rebalance your portfolio and reinvest dividends, allowing you to focus on your long-term financial objectives.

Fractional Shares: Many platforms now offer fractional shares, meaning you can invest in expensive stocks like Amazon, Tesla, or Google for as little as $1. This lowers the barrier to entry for smaller investors, allowing you to build a diversified portfolio without needing large amounts of capital.

* * *

3. Cryptocurrency and Blockchain Technology

Cryptocurrency has emerged as a new and innovative way to invest and build wealth. With the rise of Bitcoin, Ethereum, and other digital currencies, technology has opened up new opportunities for wealth creation outside of traditional markets. Blockchain technology, which underpins cryptocurrencies, has also led to the development of decentralized finance (DeFi) platforms and smart contracts that allow users to invest and transact without intermediaries.

Cryptocurrency Exchanges: Platforms like Coinbase, Binance, and Kraken provide easy access to buying, selling, and trading cryptocurrencies. They also offer educational resources to help you understand the risks and rewards of investing in digital assets.

DeFi Platforms: Decentralized finance (DeFi) platforms, such as Aave, Compound, and Uniswap, allow users to lend, borrow, and earn interest on their cryptocurrency holdings. These platforms are based on smart contracts, which are self-executing agreements coded into the blockchain, eliminating the need for intermediaries.

NFTs and Digital Assets: Non-fungible tokens (NFTs) have become a popular way to invest in digital art and collectibles. While the market for NFTs can be volatile, they present unique opportunities for creative investors looking to diversify their portfolios.

* * *

4. Automated Savings and Investment Tools

Automation has made saving and investing simpler and more effective. With automated savings tools and investment plans, you can ensure that your wealth-building efforts continue on autopilot, even when you're not actively managing them. These tools take the guesswork out of saving and investing by helping you make consistent contributions to your financial goals.

Automatic Contributions: Many investment platforms and savings accounts allow you to set up automatic contributions, so a set amount of money is transferred into your investment or savings account regularly. This strategy, known as "paying yourself first," ensures that you consistently build wealth without the temptation to spend the money elsewhere.

Round-Ups: Apps like Acorns use a feature called "round-ups" to automatically round up your purchases to the nearest dollar and invest the difference in a diversified portfolio. For example, if you buy a coffee for $3.50, the app will round it up to $4.00 and invest the 50 cents.

Smart Investment Tools: Platforms like Stash and SoFi allow you to set up automatic recurring investments in portfolios that align with your financial goals and risk tolerance. These tools offer low-cost, diversified portfolios designed to maximize your long-term returns.

* * *

5. Leveraging Financial Education and Online Resources

Technology has also democratized financial education. With access to online courses, blogs, podcasts, and financial forums, you can learn about wealth creation from experts around the world. Staying informed and continually educating yourself is key to making better financial decisions.

Online Learning Platforms: Websites like Coursera, Udemy, and Skillshare offer a wide variety of personal finance and investing courses, many of which are taught by financial professionals. These platforms provide a structured way to learn about money management, investing, and other wealth-building strategies.

Financial Blogs and Podcasts: There is an abundance of financial blogs and podcasts available for free. Blogs like The Motley Fool, Mr. Money Mustache, and The Financial Independence Podcast offer valuable insights on investing, frugality, and building wealth.

Financial Communities: Online forums and communities such as Reddit's personal finance subreddit or Bogleheads.org allow individuals to share their experiences and learn from others. These communities often provide free advice, discussions, and resources that can enhance your financial knowledge.

* * *

6. The Future of Wealth Creation: AI and Fintech Innovations

Looking ahead, the future of wealth creation is closely tied to the advancements in artificial intelligence (AI) and fintech innovations. AI-driven tools are already being used to analyze financial markets, predict trends, and provide personalized investment recommendations.

AI-Powered Investment Platforms: AI algorithms can analyze vast amounts of data to predict market trends and optimize investment portfolios. These platforms can help investors make more informed decisions by providing real-time analysis of the markets.

Fintech Innovations: The rise of fintech companies is transforming the financial landscape. With innovations like peer-to-peer lending, micro-investing, and blockchain-based insurance, fintech companies are lowering the barriers to entry and making wealth creation more accessible to everyone.

* * *

Leveraging Technology for Financial Success

Technology has become an indispensable tool in the quest for financial independence and wealth creation. By embracing financial apps, online investment platforms, automated savings tools, and educational resources, you can streamline your wealth-building efforts and maximize your financial potential. In today's digital age, those who understand how to leverage technology will be well-equipped to achieve long-term financial success. Whether you're budgeting, investing, or learning new strategies, technology is the key to unlocking your path to prosperity.

The Role of Mindful Spending

U nderstanding Mindful Spending

Mindful spending is the practice of intentionally managing
your finances to align with your personal values and long-
term financial goals. Rather than impulsively buying or following
trends, mindful spending encourages thoughtful consideration of each
purchase and its impact on your overall financial well-being. In this
chapter, we will explore how practicing mindful spending can enhance
your wealth-building efforts and help you make conscious decisions
that support your financial journey.

* * *

1. The Concept of Mindful Spending

Mindful spending involves being fully aware of how, where, and
why you spend your money. It goes beyond budgeting and focuses

on ensuring that every expenditure aligns with your priorities and financial aspirations. This practice encourages making intentional decisions that contribute to your long-term prosperity rather than immediate gratification.

Aligning Spending with Values: The first step in mindful spending is understanding your values. Are you prioritizing saving for a home? Investing in education? Or building an emergency fund? When you recognize what truly matters to you, you can direct your money toward these goals instead of wasting it on short-term desires.

Avoiding Impulse Purchases: Mindful spending requires resisting the temptation of impulse buys. By taking a moment to evaluate the necessity of a purchase and how it fits into your financial picture, you can make more informed, conscious decisions.

* * *

2. The Psychology of Spending

Understanding the psychology behind spending habits is crucial for implementing mindful spending. Many of our purchases are influenced by emotions, societal pressures, and marketing tactics. Being aware of these influences can help you avoid unnecessary spending and stay focused on your financial objectives.

Emotional Spending: Sometimes, we spend money as a way to cope with emotions like stress, sadness, or boredom. Mindful spending requires identifying emotional triggers and finding healthier ways to address these feelings without relying on purchases to fill the gap.

Social Influences and Peer Pressure: In a society that often promotes consumerism, it's easy to feel pressured to keep up with others. Mindful spending helps you separate your true needs from external influences, allowing you to spend in ways that genuinely support your goals.

Advertising and Marketing Tactics: Advertisers often create a sense of urgency or FOMO (fear of missing out) to persuade consumers to make spontaneous purchases. By recognizing these tactics, you can become more resistant to impulse buying and make purchases that truly enhance your life.

* * *

3. Creating a Mindful Spending Plan

Mindful spending requires more than just awareness; it involves actively creating and sticking to a spending plan that reflects your priorities and long-term goals.

Track Your Spending: Start by tracking where your money goes each month. Financial apps or simple spreadsheets can help you categorize and review your expenses. This will allow you to identify areas where you may be overspending on non-essential items and give you a clearer picture of how to redirect your funds toward wealth-building goals.

Set Financial Priorities: Once you've assessed your spending, set clear financial priorities. Allocate money to your essential needs, savings goals, and investments first, before considering discretionary spending. This will help ensure that your money is working toward your long-term goals.

Cutting Unnecessary Expenses: Identify areas where you can cut back on unnecessary spending, such as subscription services you don't use, impulse buys, or costly habits. By reducing these expenses, you can free up more money for investing or saving.

* * *

4. Implementing Mindful Spending in Everyday Life

Incorporating mindful spending into your daily routine requires consistency and discipline. Here are some practical strategies to help you practice mindful spending every day:

The 24-Hour Rule: Before making a non-essential purchase, implement the 24-hour rule. This means waiting at least 24 hours before making the purchase to evaluate whether it's truly necessary or if it was an impulse decision.

Mindful Shopping: When you go shopping, make a list of the items you need and stick to it. Avoid wandering through aisles or browsing online stores, as this often leads to unnecessary purchases. If you find yourself considering an item not on your list, ask yourself whether it truly adds value to your life or aligns with your goals.

Conscious Consumption: Mindful spending also involves being thoughtful about the products and services you consume. Opt for high-quality items that will last longer and provide lasting value rather than cheap, disposable products that may end up costing you more in the long run.

* * *

5. The Benefits of Mindful Spending

By practicing mindful spending, you not only improve your financial health but also develop a stronger sense of financial control and empowerment. Here are some key benefits of adopting this approach:

Increased Savings: When you consciously evaluate your spending habits, you can make room for greater savings. Redirecting money away from unnecessary purchases means more money can go toward your financial goals, such as building an emergency fund, paying off debt, or investing for the future.

Reduced Financial Stress: Mindful spending helps you gain control over your finances and reduces the anxiety that often comes from living paycheck to paycheck or relying on credit. By living within your means and prioritizing your goals, you can reduce financial stress and achieve greater peace of mind.

Improved Wealth-Building Potential: Mindful spending ensures that you are investing your money in ways that align with your wealth-building goals. This helps you create lasting wealth, as you consistently direct your resources toward building assets and growing your financial foundation.

Greater Satisfaction: By focusing on what truly matters and aligning your spending with your values, you'll find greater satisfaction in the purchases you make. You'll be more intentional about how your money is spent, and as a result, you'll feel more fulfilled with fewer, but more meaningful, possessions.

* * *

6. Mindful Spending and Long-Term Prosperity

Mindful spending is not about depriving yourself; it's about being intentional and conscious of how you use your money to support your goals. By practicing mindful spending, you create a strong foundation for long-term prosperity. Each dollar you spend becomes a reflection of your priorities, values, and financial aspirations.

Over time, this practice allows you to make decisions that not only benefit your financial future but also contribute to a more fulfilling and balanced life. Mindful spending is a powerful tool in the journey toward wealth creation, as it ensures that your financial choices are aligned with your ultimate goal: achieving lifelong prosperity.

* * *

Building Wealth with Intentional Spending

By embracing mindful spending, you ensure that every financial decision supports your wealth-building journey. Being conscious of your spending habits, aligning your purchases with your values, and eliminating unnecessary expenses will create a clear path to financial security. Remember, wealth creation isn't just about earning more; it's about making intentional decisions that allow you to grow and preserve your resources over time. With mindful spending, you are one step closer to building the life of financial independence and success that you deserve.

Building a Legacy of Wealth

The Importance of Legacy

When most people think of wealth-building, they focus on the accumulation of assets during their lifetime. However, true prosperity extends beyond personal wealth. Building a legacy of wealth ensures that the success you create today impacts not just your own life but the lives of future generations. This chapter will explore how to build a legacy that supports both your immediate family and future heirs, ensuring that the wealth you've accumulated continues to grow and benefit those who come after you.

* * *

1. Understanding Legacy Wealth

A legacy is more than just passing down financial assets. It's about leaving a lasting impact on your family, community, and the causes you care about. Building a legacy of wealth involves creating a plan that not only protects your financial resources but also ensures that your values, knowledge, and principles are passed on for generations to come.

Legacy wealth encompasses both tangible assets, such as property, investments, and cash, and intangible assets, such as wisdom, family traditions, and philanthropic values. Together, these elements create a foundation that supports future generations in their pursuit of prosperity.

Financial Legacy: This includes your monetary assets, investments, real estate, and any other physical wealth that you pass on.

Cultural and Philosophical Legacy: The values, philosophies, and knowledge that shape your family's approach to wealth-building. A legacy is also about the attitudes toward money, responsibility, and generosity that are instilled in future generations.

* * *

2. The Role of Estate Planning in Legacy Building

Creating a legacy begins with effective estate planning. Estate planning isn't just about drafting a will; it's about ensuring that your wealth is transferred in a way that minimizes taxes, legal complications, and ensures that your wishes are followed.

Wills and Trusts: A will outlines how your assets will be distributed upon your death. However, trusts allow for more control over how your wealth is distributed and when. A well-structured trust can help ensure your beneficiaries receive your assets in a manner that supports long-term growth, avoiding probate, and reducing estate taxes.

Tax Strategies: Effective estate planning includes tax strategies that minimize the impact of inheritance taxes, capital gains taxes, and other fees that could erode the wealth passed down. Understanding these strategies and working with a financial advisor can significantly increase the amount of wealth you leave behind.

Health Care Directives: Having clear health care directives ensures that your family understands your wishes regarding medical care, and can prevent confusion and unnecessary stress during difficult times.

Business Succession Plans: If you own a business, creating a succession plan is essential for ensuring the business continues to thrive after you're gone. This involves planning for the transfer of ownership, management, and operational responsibilities, helping to keep your legacy alive through your entrepreneurial endeavors.

* * *

3. Teaching Financial Literacy to Future Generations

One of the most valuable aspects of leaving a legacy is teaching financial literacy to your children, grandchildren, and even great-grandchildren. Financial knowledge empowers future generations to build upon the foundation you've created, allowing them to manage, grow, and pass on the wealth you've worked hard to accumulate.

Early Financial Education: Start teaching children the basics of managing money, saving, and investing as early as possible. Introduce them to concepts like compound interest, budgeting, and the importance of long-term financial planning.

Modeling Financial Responsibility: Children learn by example. Modeling good financial habits—such as saving regularly, budgeting, investing wisely, and avoiding debt—teaches future generations the principles of wealth-building.

Family Financial Discussions: Involve your family in financial discussions, particularly around important matters like inheritance and investments. Transparency in money management allows your heirs to understand your intentions and how to carry on the wealth-building journey.

* * *

4. Creating a Philanthropic Legacy

Another key component of building a legacy of wealth is giving back to society. Philanthropy not only enriches your life but also provides an avenue for future generations to continue your charitable efforts. Whether through charitable donations, foundations, or volunteer work, instilling a sense of giving helps ensure that your wealth has a positive impact on the world.

Establishing a Family Foundation: A family foundation is a great way to formalize your philanthropic efforts. It allows you to direct funds to causes that align with your values, while also involving your family in decision-making. This ensures that the spirit of giving is passed down.

Philanthropy as a Teaching Tool: Teaching your children and grand-children the importance of charity and generosity not only enhances their sense of purpose but also ensures that your family continues contributing to society long after you're gone.

Aligning Your Wealth with Values: Invest in causes and businesses that reflect your personal values, such as sustainable practices, educational initiatives, or local charities. This aligns your wealth with a positive social impact that your descendants can continue to support.

* * *

5. The Power of Legacy in Creating Financial Independence

A well-planned legacy not only ensures the preservation and growth of wealth but also promotes financial independence for future generations. By providing your descendants with the tools and knowledge to manage wealth responsibly, you help create a cycle of prosperity that can continue for centuries.

The Multi-Generational Approach: Building a financial legacy isn't just about passing on wealth in your will. It's about creating a multi-generational plan that includes knowledge transfer, asset protection, and philanthropic endeavors. As each generation contributes to the family's wealth, the legacy grows and strengthens.

Financial Independence for Heirs: Through effective estate planning, financial literacy, and teaching independence, you can ensure that your heirs don't rely solely on the wealth you leave behind. Instead, they'll be empowered to manage and grow it in ways that continue your legacy.

* * *

6. Leveraging Investments to Build a Legacy of Wealth

One of the most effective ways to build a lasting legacy is through long-term investments. Wealth that is invested wisely can grow exponentially, benefitting future generations for years to come. Strategic investing in stocks, bonds, real estate, and other asset classes will not only increase your wealth but provide a stable financial foundation for your heirs.

Real Estate Investments: Real estate has long been a cornerstone of wealth-building. By investing in property, you create an appreciating asset that can be passed down, along with rental income that supports future generations.

Diversified Investment Portfolios: A diversified portfolio that includes equities, fixed-income securities, and alternative investments helps ensure that your wealth continues to grow, even during market fluctuations. Long-term investments offer the potential for exponential returns, securing your family's financial future.

* * *

7. The Emotional and Cultural Impact of Legacy

The emotional aspects of building a legacy are just as important as the financial ones. The wealth you create isn't only a financial resource but a reflection of your values, your principles, and your love for your family. Instilling the importance of family unity, personal responsibility, and community contribution ensures that your legacy will be respected and carried forward by future generations.

Creating a Family Story: Every family has a unique story. Share your journey, your challenges, and your successes with your family to create a strong sense of heritage and pride. When your descendants understand the sacrifices you made and the wisdom you accumulated, they'll be more motivated to preserve and expand the legacy you've created.

Legacy Beyond Money: A legacy is not just about wealth—it's about the impact you have on those around you. Whether it's the way you lived your life, the values you instilled, or the positive changes you made in your community, these aspects of your legacy will shape how future generations remember you.

* * *

The Enduring Power of a Wealth Legacy

Building a legacy of wealth requires planning, discipline, and foresight. It's about more than just accumulating financial assets; it's about creating a plan that ensures your wealth continues to grow and benefit your family for generations to come. By investing in both tangible and intangible assets, teaching financial literacy, engaging in philanthropy, and planning for the future, you can create a legacy that outlives you and continues to inspire prosperity for those who follow in your footsteps. Your legacy of wealth will be a testament to your commitment to building a brighter future—not just for yourself, but for generations yet to come.

Health and Wealth: The Connection

The Vital Role of Health in Wealth-Building

When it comes to wealth-building, financial strategies often take center stage. However, your physical and mental well-being are just as crucial in creating lasting prosperity. Good health is the foundation for sustained success in all areas of life, including finances. This chapter explores the deep connection between health and wealth, highlighting how taking care of your body and mind can directly impact your ability to build and maintain wealth.

* * *

1. Health as an Investment

Just like financial investments, maintaining good health requires time, effort, and resources. Prioritizing your well-being is not an expense but an investment that pays dividends over the long term. When you're in good health, you're more productive, focused, and capable of making sound decisions, all of which are essential for wealth creation.

Energy and Productivity: Physical fitness increases your energy levels, making you more efficient and focused. With higher energy, you're better able to dedicate time and effort to your career, business, or investments.

Mental Clarity: Mental health and clarity directly impact your decision-making skills. A healthy mind allows you to approach business challenges and financial decisions with a clear perspective, leading to smarter and more informed choices.

* * *

2. The High Cost of Poor Health

Ignoring your health can lead to serious consequences that erode your wealth. Medical bills, lost income due to illness, and decreased productivity are just a few of the financial challenges associated with poor health.

Increased Healthcare Costs: Chronic illnesses such as diabetes, heart disease, and hypertension can lead to expensive medical treatments and medications. Preventing these conditions through a healthy lifestyle reduces long-term health expenses.

Reduced Earning Potential: Health problems can cause extended absences from work, limiting your ability to earn. Furthermore, chronic pain or illness can affect your performance, potentially leading to missed career opportunities and income loss.

Impact on Family Finances: Poor health not only affects you but can also place financial burdens on your family. Caring for a sick family member can result in lost income, higher medical costs, and emotional strain.

* * *

3. Physical Health and Wealth Creation

Maintaining physical health is critical to staying active and productive in your wealth-building endeavors. Regular exercise, balanced nutrition, and sufficient sleep can dramatically enhance your ability to create and maintain wealth.

Exercise for Longevity and Vitality: Regular physical activity not only improves your health but also helps you maintain a sharp mind and high energy. Exercise boosts your immune system, reduces stress, and enhances focus—qualities that are essential for staying productive in wealth-building pursuits.

Balanced Nutrition: What you eat directly impacts how you feel and perform. A diet rich in vitamins, minerals, and healthy fats supports cognitive function, concentration, and overall well-being, all of which contribute to your financial success.

Rest and Recovery: Sleep is an often-overlooked factor in health and productivity. Adequate sleep improves cognitive function, decision-making, and stress management, enabling you to perform at your best, both in your career and investments.

* * *

4. Mental Health: The Unsung Hero of Wealth-Building

Just as your physical health plays a vital role in wealth creation, mental health is equally important. Maintaining a positive mindset, managing stress, and fostering emotional resilience are key to navigating the challenges that come with wealth-building.

Stress Management: Financial goals often come with stress and pressure. Chronic stress can lead to burnout, poor decision-making, and even physical illness. Developing effective stress management techniques, such as meditation, yoga, or mindfulness practices, can help you stay calm and focused during challenging times.

Emotional Resilience: The road to financial success is often paved with setbacks. Developing emotional resilience allows you to recover quickly from failures and continue pushing forward with your goals. Mental health practices like therapy or self-reflection can help build emotional strength.

Positive Mindset and Motivation: A strong mental state fosters a growth-oriented mindset. With the right mindset, you're more likely to take calculated risks, overcome obstacles, and remain motivated to achieve your wealth-building objectives.

* * *

5. The Impact of Health on Long-Term Wealth Sustainability

Wealth-building is a long-term endeavor, and sustaining your wealth requires consistent effort. Good health is a critical factor in this sustainability. When you're healthy, you're more likely to maintain a consistent work ethic, make prudent decisions, and live a fulfilling life that nurtures your financial goals.

Sustaining Business Success: Entrepreneurs who prioritize their health are better equipped to handle the stresses of running a business. Maintaining energy, mental clarity, and emotional balance ensures that you can navigate the ups and downs of entrepreneurship with confidence.

Wealth Preservation: Good health increases your life expectancy, giving you more time to enjoy the wealth you've accumulated and pass it on to future generations. Healthy individuals are more likely to make sound decisions that preserve and grow their wealth over time.

* * *

6. Integrating Health into Your Wealth-Building Plan

Integrating health and wellness into your wealth-building strategy is essential for achieving true financial freedom. This integration doesn't require a drastic overhaul of your lifestyle, but rather small, consistent efforts that make a significant difference over time.

Creating a Balanced Schedule: Set aside time for exercise, meal planning, and relaxation. Balance work, leisure, and health to maintain overall well-being. This balance will improve both your health and your ability to work toward your financial goals.

Building Healthy Habits: Small habits, such as drinking water regularly, taking short walks, or practicing mindfulness, can contribute to better health and higher productivity. These habits compound over time, leading to improved physical and mental health, which ultimately supports your wealth-building efforts.

Seeking Professional Guidance: Just as you seek financial advice, consider working with health professionals such as nutritionists, personal trainers, or mental health counselors. These experts can help you optimize your health, enabling you to perform at your best both physically and financially.

* * *

7. Health and Wealth: A Symbiotic Relationship

Health and wealth are intricately connected in a symbiotic relationship. By prioritizing your health, you create the foundation for financial success. And by achieving financial success, you can access the resources needed to invest in your well-being. This cycle of health and wealth reinforces each other, leading to a prosperous, fulfilling life.

Access to Resources for Better Health: Financial success provides you with the means to afford quality healthcare, nutrition, fitness programs, and wellness services that further enhance your health, creating a positive feedback loop.

Health Enables Wealth Generation: A healthy body and mind allow you to put in the hard work necessary to build wealth. Your physical and mental state directly influence how much energy, creativity, and focus you can devote to your wealth-building activities.

* * *

A Holistic Approach to Prosperity

Health is not merely a prerequisite for wealth; it is an essential component of true prosperity. By taking care of your physical and mental well-being, you're positioning yourself for long-term financial success and personal fulfillment. A healthy body and mind provide the energy, focus, and resilience needed to overcome obstacles, make sound decisions, and sustain your wealth over time. By integrating health into your wealth-building plan, you're not only increasing your chances of financial success but also ensuring that you enjoy the benefits of your hard work for years to come.

Finding Your Wealth-Building Community

T he Power of Community in Wealth Creation

Building wealth is often portrayed as an individual journey, but the truth is that surrounding yourself with a supportive community can significantly enhance your financial success. A wealth-building community provides the motivation, knowledge, and accountability needed to stay focused on your goals. This chapter explores how to find and cultivate a community that aligns with your values and supports your pursuit of lasting wealth.

* * *

1. The Role of Community in Wealth-Building

While personal effort is essential, wealth creation is not a solitary endeavor. A strong community can provide opportunities for collaboration, learning, and growth. Whether you're an entrepreneur, investor, or someone focused on personal financial growth, having a network of like-minded individuals can elevate your journey.

Shared Knowledge and Experiences: Learning from others who are on a similar path can accelerate your growth. A community allows you to exchange tips, strategies, and insights, helping you avoid common mistakes and capitalize on successful approaches.

Emotional Support: Building wealth can be a stressful and sometimes lonely process. A supportive community offers encouragement during tough times, reminding you that setbacks are part of the journey and that success is within reach.

Accountability and Motivation: It's easy to get distracted or discouraged when working alone. A community keeps you accountable to your goals, pushing you to stay committed and take consistent action. Motivation from others can reignite your drive during moments of doubt.

* * *

2. Types of Wealth-Building Communities

Wealth-building communities come in various forms, depending on your interests and goals. Whether in person or online, you can find groups that specialize in specific wealth-building areas, such as real estate, investing, entrepreneurship, or personal finance.

Networking Groups: These are typically organized gatherings of individuals who share common financial goals. Networking groups often offer opportunities to connect with other professionals, learn from their experiences, and collaborate on projects.

Mastermind Groups: A mastermind group is a small, dedicated community of individuals who meet regularly to share knowledge, solve problems, and hold each other accountable. Being part of a mastermind group can significantly accelerate your growth by providing personalized support and feedback.

Online Communities and Forums: The internet offers a wealth of online communities centered around wealth-building topics. Websites, forums, and social media platforms allow you to connect with others across the globe, exchange ideas, and get advice from seasoned experts.

Local Wealth-Building Events: Seminars, workshops, and conferences offer opportunities to meet like-minded individuals in person. These events provide valuable educational content while fostering connections with potential collaborators and mentors.

* * *

3. How to Find a Community That Aligns With Your Goals

Not all communities are created equal. Finding the right group that matches your aspirations and values is crucial. Here are some steps to help you find your ideal wealth-building community:

Define Your Goals and Values: Before seeking out a community, take some time to clarify your own financial goals and values. Are you focused on growing your investment portfolio? Are you building a business? Do you want to improve your financial literacy? Understanding your own objectives will help you find a group that shares similar aspirations.

Look for Aligned Interests: Once you know what you're looking for, search for communities that focus on those areas. Whether it's a real estate investing group, a personal finance club, or a group for entrepreneurs, finding people who share your interests is key to building meaningful relationships.

Engage Actively: Simply joining a community is not enough. Actively engage by attending meetings, asking questions, and sharing your own experiences. By participating, you'll deepen your connections and contribute to the success of the group.

Seek Diversity in Expertise: A strong community includes individuals with diverse backgrounds and expertise. While you want a group that shares your interests, you also want to learn from people with different perspectives and skill sets. Diverse communities offer broader insights and open the door to new ideas and opportunities.

* * *

4. Benefits of Being Part of a Wealth-Building Community

The advantages of surrounding yourself with others who are also focused on wealth creation are numerous. From gaining valuable insights to creating long-lasting partnerships, being part of a community accelerates your financial journey in several ways.

Collaborative Opportunities: Communities foster collaboration, whether it's through joint ventures, partnerships, or collective problem-solving. Working with others allows you to leverage shared resources and knowledge to achieve common goals faster.

Expanded Network: A community provides access to a broader network of professionals, entrepreneurs, investors, and experts. This network can open doors to new opportunities, partnerships, and investments that you might not have encountered on your own.

Learning from Others' Successes and Failures: A community allows you to learn from both the successes and failures of others. Seeing what works and what doesn't can help you make better decisions, saving you time and money.

Increased Confidence: The support and encouragement of a like-minded community can help you overcome self-doubt and build confidence in your financial decisions. Knowing that others are on the same path and facing similar challenges gives you the strength to push forward.

* * *

5. Nurturing and Giving Back to Your Community

A thriving wealth-building community relies on its members actively contributing and supporting one another. While it's important to receive value from the community, it's equally important to give back. By sharing your experiences, insights, and successes, you contribute to the collective growth of the group.

Share Your Expertise: If you have knowledge or experience in a particular area, don't hesitate to share it with others. Whether it's offering advice on investing, providing guidance on starting a business, or sharing strategies for debt reduction, your contributions can help others on their path to financial success.

Mentorship: As you gain more experience and knowledge, consider mentoring others who are just starting their wealth-building journey. Mentorship fosters deeper connections and allows you to pay forward the support you've received.

Collaborate and Partner: Look for opportunities to collaborate with fellow community members. By pooling your resources and expertise, you can create mutually beneficial partnerships that accelerate the wealth-building process for everyone involved.

* * *

6. Overcoming Challenges in Community Building

While being part of a community offers many benefits, it's not without its challenges. Not every community will be the perfect fit, and disagreements or misalignments can arise. It's essential to remain open-minded and patient as you navigate the process of building meaningful relationships.

Finding the Right Balance: Sometimes, it may take time to find a community that truly aligns with your values and goals. Don't be discouraged by initial setbacks. Keep looking, and eventually, you'll find the right group that offers the support and growth opportunities you need.

Dealing with Negative Influences: While most communities are supportive, there may be negative influences or individuals who hinder your growth. Be discerning and remove yourself from toxic environments that do not align with your values or goals.

Building Trust: Building trust within a community takes time. Be consistent in your interactions, and focus on creating genuine connections with others. Over time, trust will develop, and the community will become a powerful asset in your wealth-building journey.

* * *

A Stronger Path to Wealth with Community Support

Surrounding yourself with a wealth-building community is one of the most powerful ways to accelerate your financial success. By learning from others, sharing your own experiences, and collaborating toward common goals, you create a strong foundation for lasting prosperity. The journey toward wealth is not a solo endeavor, and finding the right community can make all the difference in achieving your financial dreams.

Overcoming Limiting Beliefs Around Money

B reaking Free from Mental Barriers

Limiting beliefs about money can be one of the biggest obstacles on the road to financial success. These beliefs, often formed in childhood or influenced by societal views, can create subconscious barriers that prevent individuals from reaching their full wealth-building potential. This chapter explores how to identify, confront, and overcome these limiting beliefs, allowing you to shift your mindset toward attracting wealth and abundance.

* * *

1. Recognizing Limiting Beliefs About Money

Limiting beliefs are the deeply ingrained thoughts and ideas that hold you back from achieving financial success. They are often rooted in fear, insecurity, and misconceptions about money. Recognizing these beliefs is the first step toward dismantling them.

Common Limiting Beliefs: Some examples of limiting beliefs include:

"Money is hard to make."

"Rich people are greedy or corrupt."

"I don't deserve to be wealthy."

"Money doesn't grow on trees."

These beliefs can influence your behavior, leading you to avoid opportunities, settle for less, or even sabotage your financial growth without realizing it.

Identifying Your Own Beliefs: To overcome limiting beliefs, it's essential to first identify them. Reflect on your thoughts about money. Are there certain situations where you feel anxious or uncomfortable regarding money? Do you have a tendency to avoid financial decisions or feel guilty about wanting more wealth? These emotions and behaviors are often signs of limiting beliefs.

* * *

2. Understanding the Origins of Limiting Beliefs

Limiting beliefs about money are often learned early in life through experiences, cultural conditioning, and observations of those around us. Understanding where these beliefs come from can help you challenge and change them.

Childhood Influence: Many limiting beliefs are rooted in childhood, when we first begin to form our understanding of money. If you grew up in an environment where money was scarce or seen as the root of all evil, these experiences can shape how you view wealth in adulthood.

Cultural and Societal Norms: Society often perpetuates myths about money, such as the idea that wealth is only attainable through luck or inheritance, or that the pursuit of wealth is inherently negative. These societal views can cloud your judgment and create a false narrative around money.

Family and Peer Influence: The way our family members and close peers view money can also impact our beliefs. If your parents or friends held negative or limiting beliefs about money, you may have unconsciously adopted those same beliefs.

* * *

3. The Impact of Limiting Beliefs on Financial Success

Limiting beliefs can significantly hinder your ability to build wealth. When you internalize these beliefs, they create a mental block that affects your decisions, behaviors, and actions toward money.

Fear of Failure: If you believe that money is hard to come by, you may avoid taking risks or pursuing opportunities that could lead to financial growth. This fear of failure can keep you stuck in a cycle of inaction, preventing progress.

Self-Sabotage: Many individuals who struggle with limiting beliefs unknowingly sabotage their own financial success. They may avoid asking for raises, pass up investment opportunities, or remain in unsatisfying jobs because they believe they don't deserve more or that they aren't capable of achieving wealth.

Missed Opportunities: Limiting beliefs can prevent you from seeing opportunities that could propel your financial growth. You may fail to recognize the potential in investing, entrepreneurship, or career advancement because of the subconscious belief that money is out of reach.

* * *

4. Shifting Your Mindset: Embracing Abundance

The key to overcoming limiting beliefs about money is shifting your mindset from scarcity to abundance. An abundance mindset is based on the belief that there is enough wealth and opportunity for everyone, and that financial success is attainable through hard work, creativity, and perseverance.

Challenge Your Beliefs: Once you've identified your limiting beliefs, start questioning them. Ask yourself: "Is this belief really true? Is it serving me?" Consider the experiences of others who have achieved financial success and reflect on how their mindset differed from yours.

Reframe Your Thoughts: Replace limiting beliefs with empowering ones. For example, instead of thinking, "Money is hard to make," shift to, "There are many ways to create and attract wealth." Reframing your thoughts helps you open up to new possibilities and strategies for wealth-building.

Visualize Abundance: Visualization is a powerful tool for shifting your mindset. Regularly visualize yourself achieving financial success, whether it's through increasing your savings, making profitable investments, or building a thriving business. By visualizing success, you begin to believe that it's possible and start taking the necessary steps to make it a reality.

Affirmations: Use positive affirmations to reinforce your new mindset. Affirmations such as "I am worthy of financial success," "Wealth flows to me effortlessly," and "I am capable of achieving my financial goals" help retrain your subconscious mind to align with abundance.

* * *

5. Taking Action Toward Wealth Creation

Overcoming limiting beliefs is only the first step; taking consistent, proactive action is essential in creating lasting wealth. As you challenge and shift your beliefs, begin implementing strategies that align with your newfound mindset.

Set Clear Financial Goals: Break down your wealth-building journey into specific, measurable goals. Whether it's saving a certain amount, investing in assets, or building a business, setting clear goals gives you a roadmap for success.

Embrace Risk and Failure: Overcome the fear of failure by viewing it as a learning opportunity rather than a setback. Wealth creation often involves taking calculated risks and being willing to try new things, even if success isn't guaranteed right away.

Build Financial Literacy: Invest time in improving your financial knowledge. Understanding how money works and learning about investment opportunities, budgeting, and savings strategies will help you make informed decisions and take control of your financial future.

* * *

6. Surrounding Yourself with Supportive Influences

As you work on overcoming limiting beliefs, surround yourself with people who support and encourage your financial growth. Whether through mentorship, networking groups, or like-minded communities, being around individuals who share your wealth-building mindset can reinforce your progress and keep you motivated.

Seek Mentors and Role Models: Mentors who have achieved financial success can provide guidance, inspiration, and practical advice. Learning from those who have walked the path before you can help you avoid pitfalls and accelerate your journey toward wealth.

Join Wealth-Building Communities: Being part of a community of like-minded individuals helps reinforce your positive mindset and keeps you accountable to your financial goals. Sharing experiences and learning from others can provide valuable insights and new strategies for overcoming obstacles.

* * *

Embracing a Wealth Mindset for Lasting Success

Overcoming limiting beliefs around money is a crucial step toward creating lasting wealth. By challenging your old beliefs, embracing an abundance mindset, and taking actionable steps toward your financial goals, you pave the way for greater success and fulfillment. Remember, the mindset you cultivate today directly influences the wealth you create tomorrow. Keep working on your mindset, take consistent action, and watch as your financial dreams come to life.

Staying Focused on Your Long-Term Vision

The Marathon of Wealth-Building

Building lasting wealth is not a quick or easy process; it's a journey that requires patience, perseverance, and a strong focus on long-term goals. The road to financial success is filled with challenges, distractions, and setbacks. In this chapter, we explore how to stay focused on your long-term vision while managing short-term obstacles, ensuring that every step you take brings you closer to your ultimate financial goals.

* * *

1. The Importance of a Clear Vision

A clear, well-defined long-term vision is the foundation for achieving wealth. Without a vision, it's easy to become distracted by immediate gains or temporary setbacks that can veer you off course. A strong vision provides direction and motivation during challenging times, helping you stay on track toward your ultimate goals.

Setting Your Vision: Start by envisioning where you want to be financially in five, ten, or twenty years. Whether it's achieving financial independence, owning a business, or building a real estate portfolio, your vision should be specific, measurable, and meaningful to you. The clearer your vision, the easier it becomes to make decisions that align with it.

Aligning Your Goals: Break down your long-term vision into smaller, actionable goals. These can include saving a specific amount, investing in certain assets, or reaching certain milestones in your business. By aligning your daily actions with your vision, you create a roadmap that guides you toward your goals, step by step.

* * *

2. Embracing the Long-Term Journey

The journey to wealth is often slow, especially in the beginning. You may face moments of doubt or frustration, but staying committed to the process is essential. Wealth-building requires consistent effort over time, and it's important to embrace the long-term nature of the journey.

Patience Over Instant Gratification: In a world of instant rewards and quick fixes, wealth-building often feels like a slow and steady process. It's important to resist the temptation of seeking immediate results, which may be enticing but ultimately unsustainable. Trust in the process and remember that the most significant financial achievements take time.

Staying Consistent: Consistency is key. Whether it's investing regularly, saving a set percentage of your income, or growing your business every day, small, consistent actions lead to large results over time. Focus on doing the right things, day in and day out, even if the results aren't immediate.

* * *

3. Overcoming Short-Term Challenges

Throughout your wealth-building journey, you will inevitably encounter short-term challenges that threaten to derail your focus. These might include economic downturns, unexpected expenses, or changes in personal circumstances. It's important to stay resilient and keep your eye on the bigger picture, even when things seem difficult.

Adapting to Market Fluctuations: The financial markets are volatile, and downturns are inevitable. Rather than panicking or making hasty decisions, focus on your long-term strategy. Avoid the temptation to make knee-jerk reactions based on short-term market fluctuations. Stay patient and remember that long-term investments tend to recover and grow over time.

Managing Financial Setbacks: Setbacks, whether personal or financial, can happen. However, these challenges are part of the process. The key is not to dwell on them but to take proactive steps to get back on track. Adjust your strategy if necessary, but never lose sight of your ultimate goal.

Fighting Distractions: In the age of constant information and distractions, it can be difficult to stay focused. It's easy to get sidetracked by the latest financial trends, social media distractions, or even the opinions of others. Stay true to your vision and avoid being swayed by fleeting trends that don't align with your long-term goals.

* * *

4. Building Mental Toughness and Resilience

Staying focused on your long-term vision requires mental toughness and resilience. Building wealth often involves pushing through difficult moments, staying positive, and continuing to move forward, no matter the obstacles. The ability to persevere through hard times is what separates successful wealth-builders from those who give up.

Developing a Growth Mindset: A growth mindset is crucial when it comes to staying focused on your long-term vision. Instead of seeing challenges as failures, view them as opportunities to learn and grow.

Every setback is a lesson that will make you stronger and more capable of handling future obstacles.

Embracing Delayed Gratification: Delayed gratification is a core principle of wealth-building. The ability to delay immediate pleasures for long-term rewards is what enables you to stay committed to your goals. Whether it's saving money rather than spending it or forgoing short-term luxuries for future success, the ability to prioritize long-term results will pay off.

* * *

5. Celebrating Small Wins Along the Way

While staying focused on your long-term vision is crucial, it's also important to celebrate small victories along the way. Recognizing the progress you've made, no matter how small, helps maintain motivation and reinforces your commitment to your goals.

Track Your Progress: Regularly evaluate how far you've come in your wealth-building journey. Whether you've hit a savings target, made a successful investment, or paid off a debt, tracking your progress allows you to see how much you've achieved. This can give you the confidence to keep pushing forward.

Reward Yourself: Don't wait until you reach your ultimate goal to celebrate. Small rewards along the way can help keep you motivated.

Treat yourself to something meaningful when you reach a milestone, whether it's a small vacation, a special purchase, or simply taking time to acknowledge your hard work.

* * *

6. Staying Accountable and Seeking Support

Staying focused on your long-term vision is easier when you have a support system in place. Surround yourself with individuals who encourage your goals and keep you accountable for your actions.

Find a Mentor: A mentor who has already achieved the financial success you're working toward can provide invaluable guidance and perspective. Having someone who has walked the path before you can help you stay focused and avoid common pitfalls.

Join a Wealth-Building Community: Being part of a group that shares similar financial goals can keep you motivated and accountable. Whether it's an online forum, a mastermind group, or a local network of like-minded individuals, having a supportive community makes it easier to stay on track and continue your progress.

* * *

Eyes on the Prize

The journey to lasting wealth requires a clear vision, long-term dedication, and the ability to navigate challenges with resilience. By staying focused on your ultimate financial goals, you can weather the storms of short-term difficulties and stay on track toward prosperity. Remember, wealth-building is a marathon, not a sprint, and with consistent effort and a focus on the bigger picture, you will reach your destination.

Wealth-Building Habits to Adopt

The Power of Habits in Wealth Creation

The habits you cultivate today will determine your financial future. Small, consistent actions, repeated over time, compound into significant results. Individuals who achieve long-term wealth understand the importance of daily, intentional habits that set them on a path to financial success. In this chapter, we'll explore the key wealth-building habits that can transform your financial journey and help you achieve your goals.

* * *

1. Habit of Saving Consistently

Wealthy individuals prioritize saving regularly, regardless of how much they earn. They understand that saving isn't about the amount, but about the practice itself. Even small amounts saved consistently over time can accumulate into significant wealth.

Pay Yourself First: Treat saving as a non-negotiable expense. Set aside a portion of your income each month, before paying bills or spending on discretionary items. Automate savings if possible, so it's done automatically and becomes a habit.

Emergency Fund: Build an emergency fund to ensure financial security during unexpected times. Aim for three to six months' worth of living expenses to cover any financial disruptions.

* * *

2. Habit of Investing Regularly

Wealth isn't built through saving alone. Smart investing plays a crucial role. Regularly investing in assets like stocks, bonds, real estate, or mutual funds helps your money grow over time, leveraging compound interest.

Start Small, Think Long-Term: You don't need to start with large amounts. The key is consistency. Whether it's through monthly contributions to an investment account or real estate purchases, the habit of investing regularly pays off over time.

Diversify Your Portfolio: Wealthy individuals understand the importance of diversification. Spread your investments across various asset classes to mitigate risk while maximizing growth opportunities.

* * *

3. Habit of Living Below Your Means

One of the most important habits for building wealth is to avoid lifestyle inflation. As income increases, wealthy individuals often choose to live below their means, focusing on long-term financial growth instead of short-term indulgence.

Track Your Spending: Regularly monitor your expenses and create a budget. Understanding where your money goes allows you to make adjustments and identify areas for savings.

Avoid Debt: Avoid the temptation of using credit for unnecessary purchases. If debt is used, ensure it's for income-generating investments like real estate or businesses. Pay off high-interest debt as quickly as possible.

* * *

4. Habit of Continuous Learning

Wealthy individuals are lifelong learners. They constantly seek ways to expand their knowledge about finance, business, investments, and personal growth. This habit helps them make informed decisions and adapt to changing financial landscapes.

Read Books and Articles: Make a habit of reading books on personal finance, investing, and entrepreneurship. Knowledge gained from experts in these fields provides insights and strategies you can implement.

Attend Seminars and Workshops: Participate in seminars or workshops related to wealth-building strategies. Networking with experts and peers can expose you to new ideas and investment opportunities.

* * *

5. Habit of Goal Setting and Tracking Progress

Setting clear financial goals is essential. Wealthy individuals don't leave their financial success to chance; they set specific, measurable, and achievable goals. Tracking progress helps maintain focus and motivates them to stay on track.

SMART Goals: Set financial goals that are Specific, Measurable, Achievable, Relevant, and Time-bound. Break them into smaller, actionable steps, and track your progress regularly.

Review and Adjust: Evaluate your progress at regular intervals. If you're not on track, adjust your strategies. Financial success isn't about perfection; it's about consistency and making course corrections when necessary.

* * *

6. Habit of Networking and Building Relationships

Building relationships with other like-minded individuals can accelerate wealth creation. Wealthy people understand the power of networking and actively surround themselves with successful people who can open doors to opportunities and provide valuable advice.

Attend Networking Events: Join events where you can meet successful individuals. Surround yourself with people who share your values and financial goals.

Build Strong Relationships: Focus on building authentic, mutually beneficial relationships rather than just seeking personal gain. Long-term, genuine connections lead to valuable opportunities.

* * *

7. Habit of Patience and Discipline

Wealth-building is a long-term endeavor. Patience and discipline are critical habits for staying focused on your financial goals, even when the results are not immediate. Wealthy individuals understand that it takes time to build significant wealth.

Resist Impulse Spending: Wealthy individuals practice delayed gratification. They avoid the temptation to make impulsive purchases and instead invest in opportunities that yield long-term returns.

Stick to Your Plan: Don't be swayed by the latest financial trends or get-rich-quick schemes. Stay disciplined, keep following your plan, and trust the process.

* * *

8. Habit of Giving Back

Wealthy individuals often practice generosity and give back to their communities. This habit not only has a positive impact on others but also helps cultivate an abundance mindset. When you share, you open yourself to receiving more in return.

Charity and Giving: Set aside a portion of your income or time to give to causes that align with your values. Giving fosters a sense of purpose and satisfaction that goes beyond financial wealth.

Mentorship: Wealthy individuals often mentor others, sharing their knowledge and experiences to help others succeed. Helping others grow can create lasting connections and support your own journey.

* * *

9. Habit of Embracing Technology

In today's digital age, using technology to manage finances and investments is essential. Wealthy individuals understand the importance of staying updated on technological advancements and utilizing tools that streamline wealth-building processes.

Use Financial Apps: Leverage budgeting, investing, and expense-tracking apps to monitor and manage your finances effectively.

Research Opportunities Online: Technology provides access to a wide range of investment opportunities. Use online platforms and resources to stay informed about market trends, investment tools, and potential income streams.

* * *

The Path to Financial Success

Wealth-building isn't an overnight achievement. It's the result of consistent habits, practiced over time. By adopting the wealth-building habits outlined in this chapter—saving consistently, investing regularly, living below your means, and continuously learning—you can set yourself up for long-term financial success. Remember, habits shape your future. By cultivating the right habits now, you'll pave the way for a lifetime of wealth.

The Power of Giving Back

The True Measure of Wealth

Wealth is often viewed as the accumulation of assets, but true prosperity extends far beyond financial success. Giving back to others, whether through time, money, or resources, is a powerful way to enhance your wealth, both personally and in the broader community. In this chapter, we explore how the act of giving not only benefits others but also helps to expand and solidify your own financial well-being.

* * *

1. The Ripple Effect of Generosity

Generosity can create a ripple effect that extends well beyond your initial act of giving. By sharing your resources with others, you contribute to the well-being of those around you, fostering a cycle of support and abundance.

Positive Impact: Whether it's contributing to a cause, supporting a family member, or investing in a local business, your generosity helps create opportunities for others. This builds a community of prosperity that you're part of.

Building Stronger Relationships: Giving also strengthens relationships. When you invest in the success and happiness of others, you build deeper connections and trust, which can lead to opportunities in your own financial journey.

* * *

2. Enhancing Your Mindset of Abundance

A key element of wealth-building is developing a mindset of abundance. Generosity plays a crucial role in shifting your focus from scarcity to abundance. When you give freely, you remind yourself that there is always enough to share, which allows you to continue attracting wealth and opportunities.

Opening Yourself to More: Giving fosters the belief that the more you share, the more you will receive. This mindset attracts wealth because it shifts your focus from "what if I run out" to "there's always enough."

Gratitude and Fulfillment: Generosity brings a sense of fulfillment and gratitude, which enhances your overall happiness. Wealth is not just about accumulating material assets but about enjoying the richness of life, including the joy of giving.

* * *

3. The Financial Benefits of Philanthropy

While giving may seem like a sacrifice, it can actually have financial benefits. Philanthropy, when practiced strategically, can lead to tax benefits, networking opportunities, and even investment returns.

Tax Deductions: Donations to charitable organizations often come with tax incentives, which can reduce your tax burden and help you preserve more wealth for future investments.

Networking and Influence: Being involved in philanthropic efforts can connect you with influential individuals and organizations. These relationships can create opportunities in business, investment, and other areas of wealth-building.

Legacy Creation: Giving back also allows you to create a lasting legacy. Establishing a charity, fund, or scholarship in your name ensures that your wealth continues to benefit others long after you've passed.

* * *

4. Creating a Giving Strategy

Philanthropy can be most impactful when approached with intention. Developing a giving strategy ensures that your contributions align with your values and financial goals, allowing you to make a lasting difference.

Identify Causes You Care About: Whether it's education, poverty alleviation, or environmental sustainability, identify causes that resonate with you. Your genuine passion for these areas will help you make a meaningful impact.

Set a Giving Budget: Just like saving or investing, giving should be a planned part of your financial strategy. Set aside a percentage of your income or assets each year for charitable purposes, and commit to giving regularly.

Involve Your Family: Wealth-building and giving can be a family endeavor. Involve your children or loved ones in the process of charitable giving, teaching them the importance of contributing to the greater good.

* * *

5. The Joy of Giving

The ultimate reward of generosity is the joy it brings. Wealth is about more than just financial freedom—it's about living a life of purpose, joy, and contribution. Giving back allows you to experience the satisfaction of knowing that you are making a difference in the world, while simultaneously enhancing your own prosperity.

Feel Good Factor: Studies show that giving increases happiness. The act of helping others fosters feelings of accomplishment, satisfaction, and emotional well-being, all of which contribute to a more fulfilling life.

Giving as a Lifestyle: Wealthy individuals often practice giving as part of their lifestyle. Whether it's through donations, time, or mentorship, giving back becomes a natural and integrated part of their wealth journey.

* * *

6. The Power of Collective Giving

While individual giving is powerful, collective efforts can have an even greater impact. Joining forces with like-minded individuals or organizations allows you to make a larger impact and create systemic change.

Philanthropic Networks: Many wealthy individuals join networks or clubs dedicated to philanthropy, where they pool resources and work together to address complex issues in society. These collective efforts can bring about lasting change and significantly expand your influence.

Community Involvement: By engaging with your local community and supporting grassroots initiatives, you can contribute to real change on a more personal level. Your actions, no matter how small, can inspire others to join in and create a broader movement of giving.

* * *

7. Giving as a Long-Term Wealth-Building Tool

Generosity isn't just about giving away money—it's a long-term wealth-building tool. By establishing a habit of giving, you create a life of abundance, attract new opportunities, and build relationships that can help you grow your wealth.

Investing in People: When you give, you invest in others. This investment can lead to unexpected opportunities, partnerships, and returns that benefit you in ways that monetary accumulation cannot.

Spiritual and Emotional Wealth: Giving enriches your spirit and emotional life, fostering a sense of fulfillment and purpose that contributes to your overall well-being. The wealth of joy, gratitude,

239

and connection that comes from giving is often more meaningful than financial success alone.

* * *

Wealth Beyond Money

True wealth is measured not by what you accumulate, but by how you use your resources to improve the lives of others. The power of giving back allows you to create a legacy of abundance, impact, and fulfillment. By practicing generosity, you expand your own wealth, build stronger relationships, and contribute to the prosperity of those around you. In the end, the more you give, the more you will receive— not just in material wealth, but in life's greatest riches: joy, purpose, and fulfillment.

Celebrating Your Wealth Journey

Reflecting on Your Path

The pursuit of wealth is not just about accumulating assets— it's about the journey you take, the lessons you learn, and the person you become along the way. As you reach milestones and achieve your financial goals, it's important to pause, reflect, and celebrate. This final chapter serves as a reminder that wealth is a continuous journey, not a final destination. By recognizing your progress and appreciating the steps you've taken, you empower yourself to keep going.

* * *

1. Acknowledging Your Progress

Building wealth is a long-term endeavor, and it's easy to get caught up in the chase for more. However, it's essential to celebrate the small wins and the milestones that mark your journey. Each step forward is a testament to your commitment, discipline, and perseverance.

Small Victories Matter: Whether it's paying off debt, saving your first $10,000, or successfully making your first investment, each achievement brings you closer to your overall goal. Take the time to appreciate these moments.

Progress Over Perfection: Remember, wealth-building is not a perfect process. There will be challenges, setbacks, and lessons learned. Focus on progress, not perfection, and celebrate how far you've come.

* * *

2. The Value of Self-Reflection

As you reflect on your wealth journey, it's important to take stock of the personal growth that has occurred along the way. Wealth-building is as much about developing the right mindset and habits as it is about accumulating assets. The lessons you've learned, the discipline you've developed, and the resilience you've built are all invaluable components of your success.

Identify Growth Areas: Reflect on how your mindset and financial habits have evolved. How has your understanding of money, investing, and saving shifted over time? This self-reflection deepens your connection to your journey.

Embrace the Challenges: Every challenge faced is a lesson learned. Even financial setbacks have taught you something valuable. Celebrate your ability to adapt, learn, and move forward.

* * *

3. Gratitude for Your Achievements

Gratitude is an essential practice for sustaining long-term wealth. When you are grateful for the journey and the opportunities it has brought you, you begin to attract more of what you desire. Gratitude also enhances your overall well-being, which is a cornerstone of true wealth.

Appreciate Your Resources: Take a moment to be thankful for the resources you've had, whether it's your financial knowledge, your support network, or your ability to overcome obstacles. These resources are what have helped you reach your milestones.

Celebrate Your Support Network: No one achieves success alone. Whether it's mentors, family, friends, or colleagues, acknowledge those who have supported and encouraged you along the way. They've played a pivotal role in your wealth journey.

* * *

4. Staying Humble and Grounded

While it's important to celebrate your success, staying humble and grounded is key to continuing your journey. The wealth you've accumulated is a reflection of your hard work and dedication, but it's important to remember that your success is not solely defined by material possessions.

Wealth is Not Just Money: True wealth encompasses all aspects of life, including health, relationships, personal growth, and emotional well-being. Celebrate your wealth in every form it takes.

Give Back: As you celebrate your success, continue to give back. Share your wisdom, time, and resources with others who are on a similar journey. This generosity enhances your own wealth and keeps you connected to your community.

* * *

5. Setting New Milestones for the Future

The celebration of your current achievements is not an end, but a starting point for new goals and opportunities. The journey to wealth is ongoing, and once you've reached one milestone, it's time to set the next. The key to continued success is to keep evolving, learning, and growing.

Create New Financial Goals: Use your accomplishments as a springboard to create new and even more ambitious financial goals. Your wealth-building journey is never truly complete as long as there are new opportunities to explore.

Keep the Momentum Going: Success breeds success. As you celebrate your current wealth, think about the next level of financial freedom you want to achieve. Set your sights higher and use the momentum of your past achievements to propel you forward.

* * *

6. The Importance of Celebrating Life's Journey

Wealth is more than financial security; it's about living a life of purpose, fulfillment, and joy. Celebrating your journey allows you to appreciate the richness of your life beyond material wealth. It's about finding balance, enjoying the present, and looking forward to what lies ahead.

Enjoy the Present: While working toward your financial goals, don't forget to enjoy the journey. Life's greatest wealth often lies in the moments of joy, connection, and growth along the way.

Live Your Legacy: As you celebrate your wealth, remember that the true legacy of your wealth-building journey is the impact it has on others. The positive influence you have on your family, community, and the world around you is the most lasting wealth you can create.

* * *

The Continuous Journey of Wealth

Your wealth journey is a lifelong process, not a destination. As you celebrate your milestones, reflect on the lessons learned, express gratitude for your progress, and look forward to the future. Wealth-building is a continual evolution, and the key to true success is in the ongoing pursuit of growth, generosity, and fulfillment. Keep celebrating your journey, stay grounded, and always be open to the endless possibilities that lie ahead.

A Journey of Lifelong Prosperity

As you close the pages of this book, remember that the journey to wealth is not defined by the destination but by the steps you take every day toward building a brighter, more prosperous future. The principles shared within these chapters—from mastering your finances to cultivating a wealth-building mindset—are not mere theories, but actionable strategies you can implement immediately.

We've explored the foundational steps of wealth creation, from understanding financial literacy to making smart investment choices. We've discussed how to build a solid financial base, develop income streams, and protect your wealth. We've seen how discipline, patience, and mindful spending are crucial to staying on track. And we've also touched on the importance of giving back, networking, and staying true to your long-term vision.

But perhaps the most important lesson to take away is this: wealth is a holistic journey. It's not only about accumulating money but about creating a life of purpose, fulfillment, and legacy. True prosperity is achieved when your financial success aligns with your personal values, health, and relationships.

By applying the wisdom shared in this book, you've already taken the first steps toward lifelong prosperity. Now, the next chapter is yours to write. Remember, the pursuit of wealth is not about perfection—it's about progress. It's about being resilient in the face of setbacks, staying focused on your goals, and continuously growing into the best version of yourself.

As you continue your wealth-building journey, know that every decision you make and every habit you cultivate brings you closer to the life you envision. Keep moving forward with confidence, knowing that the principles of financial success are in your hands. This is not the end, but the beginning of your ongoing pursuit of wealth and abundance.

Stay committed. Stay focused. And above all, celebrate every step of the way, knowing that prosperity is not just something you achieve— but something you live.

* * *

Thank you for joining me on this journey. May this book serve as a lasting guide and a source of motivation as you continue your path toward lasting wealth and prosperity.

www.ingramcontent.com/pod-product-compliance
Lightning Source LLC
Chambersburg PA
CBHW071448220526

45472CB00003B/724